TOOLS AND IDEAS

TOOLS AND IDEAS

The Beginnings of Local Industrialization in South Gujarat, 1970–2000

HEIN STREEFKERK

MANOHAR
2006

First published 2006

The editing and production costs were partly funded by
the 'Netherlands Organisation for Scientific Research' (NWO)

ISBN 81-7304-693-X

Published by
Ajay Kumar Jain *for*
Manohar Publishers & Distributors
4753/23 Ansari Road, Daryaganj
New Delhi 110 002

Printed at
Lordson Publishers Pvt Ltd
Delhi 110 007

Distributed in South Asia by
FOUNDATION
BOOKS
4381/4, Ansari Road
Daryaganj, New Delhi 110 002
and its branches at Mumbai, Hyderabad,
Bangalore, Chennai, Kolkata

To
Arni, my wife
and
in memory of
Tessa and Marte,
our daughters

Contents

FOREWORD

This book by Hein Streefkerk is a study of industrial development and labour relations in Gujarat in western India. It is based on several periods of fieldwork in the countryside of south Gujarat between 1970 and 2000. The findings presented in this book provide an in-depth analysis of the different phases of industrialization in Gujarat, covering both the period of planned development and that of the more recent phase of economic liberalization. Since many years, Gujarat is one of the most industrialized states of India. This applies especially to the 'golden corridor' between Ahmedabad and Mumbai, in which also Bulsar district—the fieldwork location of this book—is situated. At the same time, the economic success of this part of India has been accompanied by structural poverty among large sections of the population. Entrepreneurial spirit has progressed together with a worsening of labour conditions in various respects, among them a casualization of the labour force. In short, economic change in south Gujarat is an illustration of a contradictory model of development and deprivation, as is shown in this long-term study of industrialization and labour relations in Bulsar district.

This publication by Hein Streefkerk is one of a long line of books on Gujarat society by scholars from the University of Amsterdam. Academic interest in Gujarat society started with a first group of Dutch doctoral candidates who came to India in 1962, among them Jan Breman, Klaas van der Veen, Chris Baks and Enno Hommes. This first generation of Dutch scholars on Gujarat society initiated a second research project in the early 1970s on processes of social change in south Gujarat, which had a strong collaboration component with Indian counterparts built into it. This collaborative effort resulted, among other things, in a joint publication edited by S. Devadas Pillai and Chris Baks, entitled *Winners and Losers: Styles of Development and Change in an Indian Region* (Mumbai, 1979).

As part of this Indo-Dutch research project, Hein Streefkerk came to south Gujarat in 1971 to conduct fieldwork for his doctoral thesis, along with Loes Schenk-Sandbergen and Hans Schenk. He took upon himself to study the development of modern small-scale industry in Bulsar district and to focus on the aspects of entrepreneurship and labour relations. This research resulted in a book entitled *Industrial Transition in Rural India: Artisans, Traders and Tribals in South Gujarat* (Mumbai, 1985). As part of the second generation of Dutch scholars on Gujarat society, Hein Streefkerk has actively stimulated various new research projects on Gujarat by younger scholars since then, while he continued to conduct empirical research in the region himself. Partly through his efforts, over the past 40 years, a large number of MA theses and as many as 12 Ph.D. theses have been completed at the University of Amsterdam on Gujarat alone, while two Ph.D. theses are in progress at the moment.

Over the years, Hein Streefkerk has had a special interest in topics related to research methodology in the field of anthropology. He has written extensively on the issue of the researcher as research instrument, being a major feature of socio-anthropological fieldwork. A selection of these articles were published earlier in a volume of essays entitled *On the Production of Knowledge: Fieldwork in South Gujarat, 1971-1991* (Amsterdam, 1993). In these essays he emphasizes that the gathering of data, their analysis, and evaluation are highly sensitive to the personality, perception and theories of the fieldworker. It causes divergent representations and valuations of the same processes and phenomena by different researchers, and sometimes even different interpretations of the same subject by the same fieldworker over the years. This last issue is rarely discussed in the literature. In this new book, however, Hein Streefkerk gives an open and detailed account of the reasons why he had to change his earlier opinion on industrial entrepreneurship in Bulsar.

This book, therefore, not only covers a thirty year period of change in Gujarat society but it also deals with a thirty year period of change in the perception and analytical perspective of a researcher. Being part of the third generation of Dutch scholars on Gujarat society, I consider it an honour to write this preface to Hein Streefkerk's new book. He is a scholar who shows a sincere personal interest in the ups and down of the family of colleagues and always urges them to balance academic work and family life. Just after he had completed the manuscript of this book in the summer of 2004, and only one month before his formal retirement, Hein Streefkerk was struck by a viral infection which partly affected his nervous system. Since then his condition has improved to a large extent, although full recovery is still some way off. The stream of colleagues and ex-students who continue to visit him, along with friends and family members, clearly shows the personal touch to academic work that he has been practising over the years.

I would like to thank the Netherlands Organization for Scientific Research (NWO) for their financial support and to Mrs F. Grootoonk especially who took a keen interest in the production of the book. Finally, I would like to express my gratitude to Manohar Publishers, especially to Mr Ramesh Jain for the accuracy and speed with which he and his editorial staff completed this publication.

Department of Sociology and Anthropology
University of Amsterdam

MARIO RUTTEN

INTRODUCTION

This book deals with owners and workers in the workshops and factories of south Gujarat. It spans a period of 30 years, from 1970–2000. It describes the transformation of a predominantly rural area into an industrial belt. I began studying the process in 1971,[1] and made my final observations in 1998. I started my research in the sub-district (taluka)[2] of Bulsar. Today the taluka and the district of Bulsar are part of Gujarat's 'Golden Corridor'. In 1970, the area was known for its mangoes[3] and grasslands. Grass was sold to the buffalo stables in Andheri, Mumbai. Surnames like Ghaswala (grass merchant), the name of a prominent family in Bulsar, are reminders of the rural past of the town. 'Golden Corridor' is the name of the coastal zone that starts at the southernmost end of Gujarat, in the industrial town of Vapi. The zone terminates 200 km to the north of Vapi, in the city of Baroda. Vapi and Baroda, and the city of Surat, which lies in between these two, are on the Western Railway Line, which connects Mumbai in the south with New Delhi in the north. In the past decade, Gujarat's economic growth has been concentrated in this strip, and its growth has been similar to the 'Asian tiger' economies (*The Economist,* 2001).

The fame of the zone is age-old. It is part of Gujarat's west coast, which in the past had been one of India's major economic regions. The area achieved considerable degree of commercialization long before the establishment of British rule. Its inhabitants had long ago developed long-distance trade with Africa, Europe, and several Asian countries. Initially, the heart of its economic life was in the cities of Cambay and Bharuch at the northern end of coastal Gujarat. They were main ports and centres of manufacture before the city of Surat rose to prominence around 1600.

The book also narrates the history of social science discourse on the basis of my search for a way to understand what I observed. Initially, at the beginning of my research in the 1970s, I was influenced by the *modernization theory*, the dominant sociological explanation for economic development. It identifies industrialization with 'development', and both with modernization. Modernization theory includes a group of approaches rooted in the works of Tönnies (1855–1936), Durkheim (1858–1917), and Weber (1864–1920). Tönnies and the others witnessed the dawning of rapid industrialization and the modern age and tried to understand the radical changes in their world. They perceived these changes with ambivalence rather than as first steps towards a new age of progress. The ideas of Marx (1818–83), which I will discuss later in this chapter, were based on the same experiences, ambivalence, and concerns.[4]

In retrospect, Tönnies and his contemporaries tried to understand what is now called *capitalist modernization* and *capitalist modernity*. They saw the capitalist mode of production breaking through the tributary mode and mercantilist domination (Wolf, 1982: 266). This breakthrough was achieved first in England in the second half of the eighteenth century. It occurred in Germany and France in the nineteenth century.[5] The spread of the capitalist mode set in motion global flows of commodities and large-scale movements of people towards developing centres of industrial activity (Wolf, 1982). Great thinkers like Marx and Weber witnessed rationalization and bureaucratization. They experienced rising nationalism and emerging nation-states. They observed the movement of villagers to towns and cities and the origins of urban poverty. They speculated about changing beliefs and feelings. Last but not the least, they saw the manufacture of goods in factories on a massive scale, with machines powered first by water and firewood and later by fossil-fuels.

Durkheim studied the problem of social cohesion. He posited that pre-industrial societies cohere because of their mechanical solidarity, which is based on interpersonal bonds of neighbourhood and kinship. It led to tightly connected communities, which were broken down by the emergence of industrial society. He perceived division of labour as an integrating force in modern societies because it caused interdependence, or organic solidarity. Tönnies developed identical concepts of *Gemeinschaft* and *Gesellschaft*, or community and association to characterize pre-industrial and industrial societies, or tradition and modernity. For Weber it was more the process of progressive rationalization, or *Entzauberung* (disenchantment) that was at the root of industrialization in European history. The importance of the new Protestant ethic in the origin of modern capitalism was another theme he analysed while exploring the rise of capitalism in Europe. In 1905 he postulated the relationship between religion, its everyday ethics, and the rise of capitalist industrialization.[6] Study of secondary sources led him to conclude that, unlike the other-worldly asceticism of Hinduism, Calvinist inner-worldly ascetics promoted industrial capitalism.

The *fin de siècle* studies of Durkheim, Weber, Tönnies, and their contemporaries were attempts to comprehend the transforming European world between 1850 and 1900. The argument necessitates to add that in South Asia and Japan, urbanization and capitalist industrialization occurred in the same period, though on a much smaller scale. The population of Mumbai rose from 234,032 in 1833 to 773,195 in 1891 (Farooqui, 1996: 2,750; Tindall, 1992: 190). Other cities in South Asia, such as Ahmedabad, Karachi, Kolkata and Dacca, expanded too (Gadgil, 1973; 149, 152, 153). The 25 years between 1850 and 1875 saw the beginnings of factories in South Asia (Gadgil: 195). Gujarat was the only part of India where industry had been developed by Indian resources to any considerable extent. Its enterprising class of traders (Banias) had carried on commerce with foreign countries from ancient times (Gadgil: 198).

In the 1950s the opinions of Durkheim and Weber were taken as ways to solve problems of poverty and slow economic growth in Asia, Africa, and Latin America. Official recognition during the Second World War preceded the increased international prestige of the young European and American study of sociology. The US War Department studied the morale of the American soldier (Stouffer, 1949), and Ruth Benedict (1946) Japanese culture and personality. Meanwhile, faith in social scientists as planners and social engineers increased (Mannheim, 1940).

For many scholars, planners, and politicians, including Nehru (1956), industrialization was synonymous with development, which was the path to growth and emergence from backwardness. Theories and speculations about social conditions for economic growth and industrialization borrow heavily from Durkheim and Tönnies. One series of theories explained the differences between the pre-industrial world and the modern world in terms of the social prominence of 'status' in the pre-modern world versus the importance of 'contract' in modern societies. Other analyses were inspired by Weber. These emphasized the importance of capitalist entrepreneurship and elaborated on the conditions under which it would unfold.

The American sociologist Parsons (1955) is an exponent of the first. He developed a scheme which has been used to explain differences between tradition and modernity. His scheme included the well-known twin concepts like particularism-universalism, and ascription-achievement. Development entailed a social shift, both cause and consequence of industrialization, from particularism to universalism, or from ascription to achievement. He meant that modernization implied a change from status and prestige based on birth, towards status and prestige individually earned by education or economic success. His argument was that, for instance, finding a job in the modern world is based on skills rather than on ties of the employer with the applicant's father or cousin.

The two best known representatives of the entrepreneurial perspective are Rostow (1960), with his 'take-off into self-sustained growth', and the Harvard psychologist McClelland (1961) with his theory of achievement motivation. Rostow's airplane metaphor implied that there would be a 'take-off' following the traditional, transitional, and maturity stages. The take-off stage would be dedicated to mass consumption and armament. Entrepreneurs were supposed to contribute to the acceleration of economic growth. 'What appears to be required for the emergence for such (entrepreneurial) elites . . . (is) first, the new elite must feel itself denied the conventional routes to prestige and power . . . (s)econd the traditional society must be sufficiently flexible, or weak, to permit its members to seek material advance' (in Higgins: 223).

Weber's ideas inspired McClelland's achievement theory. The presence of a specific motivational structure, the desire to achieve, purely for achievement, that is, the achievement motivation, is of critical importance. Hagen (1962) attributes an important role to personality factors as well. He argues that a creative personality is a requirement for technical innovation. Such a personality type, according to Hagen, cannot surface in a traditional society characterized by an authoritarian personality type. Unlike McClellands's theory, Hagen's has a social component. The desired creative personality type will develop in those groups which have undergone a drop in their social status. Consequently his view belongs to those sociological approaches in which the existence of innovative economic behaviour is reduced to the specific position of the innovating group vis-à-vis other groups.

Hoselitz (1960) is an exponent of this argument. He points out to the important contribution to economic development made by culturally marginal groups. Members of such group are pre-eminently in a position to actualize innovations as a result of their ambiguous social and cultural position (Hoselitz: 66). Clifford Geertz (1963) also attributes an important role to the group's changed social status. He posits that innovating groups will spring forth from those categories which have undergone radical changes in their relations with their environment. The uncertainty in status which results from such changes can lead to economic innovation. Geertz further maintains that entrepreneurship will develop in clear-cut homogeneous groups and that such groups are characterized by a long existing 'extra-village status and inter local orientation' (Geertz: 147-50).

Young (1971) proceeds from a combination of Hagen's and Geertz's ideas in an approach which is also closely related to that of Hoselitz. He sees in the interrelation between minority status and the internal solidarity resulting from it, an important determinant for the emergence of entrepreneurship.

I felt ill at ease with the literature of the modernization authors.[7] I considered them too ethnocentric and did not agree with their emphasis on psycho-cultural characteristics. African and Asian people were characterized as lacking psychological qualities present in Europeans and Americans. Potential entrepreneurs missed the proper motivation, and factory workers lacked an industrial attitude, their commitments were said to be in the village instead of the factory.

Fieldwork confirmed my doubts. The literature did not offer me an internal framework for analysing the developments in Bulsar. I found that during the 1940s and 1950s, artisans began to manufacture the wooden bobbins and spools used by the Indian textile industry. They were the first in Bulsar to start industrial operations. In the 1960s these artisans were supplanted as major industrialists by former shopkeepers, moneylenders, rice, grain, and timber merchants. Some had migrated from Mumbai, others belonged to prominent local families. In this second batch of industrialists, Jain and Vaishnava

Banias were the single largest group of owners. They owned one-third of the industrial undertakings. Among the other proprietors were Anavils and Patidars. Banias have been the pre-eminent traders and businessmen in and outside Gujarat. Anavils and Patidars have traditionally been the dominant land-owning castes in south and central Gujarat and are politically very influential. These people owned and managed industrial firms, producing a range of products such as plastics, switches, stationery, synthetic textiles, chemicals, cardboard products, paints, elevators, electrical motors, and engineering products. The number of workers in these establishments varied between 15 and 50. Some companies employed even more than 50 workers, but only a few had more than 100 workers.

Leading modernization ideas about the psychological and social conditions required for industrial entrepreneurship to develop did not really shed any light. Old and new industrialists did not belong to socially marginal groups, nor did their groups suffer from status deprivation or status uncertainties. Above all, entrepreneurial efforts in south Gujarat were not individual phenomena.[8] Typically, the joint family was the ideal and the organizational principle behind industrial enterprises, which invalidated a highly individualist psychological approach to understanding local entrepreneurship. There was nothing exceptional nor mysterious about industrial entrepreneurs in Bulsar; their rise was obvious.

The first generation of industrialists, Suthars and Luhars, Carpenters and Blacksmiths, emerged during the Second World War. Declining imports and the need for supplying the Indian army caused production of Indian textiles to increase, while ending the imports of Japanese bobbins led to increased demand for wooden bobbins and spools. Carpenters and blacksmiths used their abilities to work with wood and metal to produce these articles. They had the skills and were not afraid to produce for distant and anonymous customers. Furthermore, the initial financial requirements to produce mechanically large quantities were relatively lower. Joint family, kin, *jati*[9] *bhaio* (people from the same caste) and friends were an important social reservoir for loyal, inexpensive labour, finance, and information. From the mid-1930s onwards, decentralized sources of power such as light diesel motors and electrical motors enabled artisans to manufacture their products industrially in home workshops or adjacent small sheds. The second group of industrialists belonged to the most prominent socio-economic and political groups locally and in the state of Gujarat. Their access to administrators, sources of funding technological expertise, raw materials, and customers seemed of fundamental import to their entrepreneurial success.

Workers in these factories were almost all first generation industrial workers. They were usually employed in a temporary capacity. The great majority was marginal or landless peasants that lived in surrounding villages, and these workers were notable more for their subordinate and compliant attitude than for their lack of commitment.

To analyse the conditions and processes more adequately, it was important to study 'power and politics'.[10] The social anthropology of Bailey (1969) and Boissevain (1974) was of help. They showed how to study strategies and coalitions of individuals who compete for influence and struggle to maximize power. They described how people use their *social networks* strategically, and emphasized the importance of *non-groups* such as *leaders and followers* (Boissevain, 1974).

The upsurge of Marxist and Marxist-inspired literature in the 1960s and early 1970s was even more helpful. To understand the origin and features of European capitalist industrialization, Marx formulated the social division of classes and class struggles that shaped history and caused social change. He also believed that economic class determined individual and collective behaviour. It is a central tenet in his theories. He asserted that the common location within the production process (*Klasse an sich*), led incumbents to acquire a common consciousness of their situation (*Klasse für sich*) Marxist-inspired authors like Frank (1967), Baran (1968), Bettelheim (1971), and Wallerstein (1974) described the origin of global markets, metropoles and satellites, unequal exchanges, pointing to the structural causes of underdevelopment.

After reading these works, I was able to see how political and economic conditions determined entrepreneurial behaviour. For instance, during my fieldwork in 1971, I discovered the *commercialism* of the new industrialists, which is the inclination to spread investments over diverse commercial and productive activities. Earlier writers like Buchanan (1966: 146), Hoselitz (1960: 151), Hazlehurst (1966: 145), and Fox (1968: 143)[11] signalled this tendency, blaming it on the traders' reluctance to invest in productive enterprises and their highly developed profit motivation.[12]

I reasoned that commercialism had not been caused by the new industrialists' psychological make-up, but was rather a result of structural constraints. These included the relatively limited size of the Indian market because of a decline of purchasing power among the rural population in the 1960s and 1970s, as well as limited export possibilities. The limited market led to channelization of capital to the non-productive sphere and encouraged spreading risks and a succession of productive and commercial activities. This economy required access to a variety of scarce resources, which was the privilege of politically or economically influential groups.

Likewise, I was able to understand and better analyse labour conditions and workers' compliance. Material contradictions explained their lack of unity and weak resistance to the appalling conditions in the small factories.

After 1985 I became convinced that the Western intellectual perception of Asia and the scholarship on industrialization and entrepreneurship in particular had been influenced by Orientalism[13] (Said, 1978). During the last decades, ever more material has been made available on early South Asian commercial ventures. For instance, Dale (1994: 1-7) writes about Indian world economy between 1500 and 1700 and the widespread dispersal of tens of thousands of Indian merchants over Indian trade diaspora in Iran, Turan and Russia, like the Caspian port Astrakhan. He observes technical and organizational resemblances between Indian merchants, like the Jains and Marwaris, and their well-known contemporaries in Genoa, Florence and Siena between 1600–1750. He also points to similarities of the palazzo-like houses (*havelis*) of Banias and those of the Italian Renaissance merchants of Genoa and Venice. These *havelis* can still be found in Indian cities. They appear to be architectural reminders of those similarities (Dale: 135).

I also began to realize that the modernization approaches and Marxist views had much in common. In the 1970s, Marxist viewpoints were an innovation from the dominant sociology of modernization, but the two perspectives also shared important similarities. One similarity was the conviction of their scholarly grandfathers, Marx and Weber, that the civilizations of the West were superior to eastern civilizations such as the Hindu. They believed that the inhabitants of the South Asian peninsula would not be able to effectuate capitalist industrialization. In 1853, Marx wrote of the 'sensualist exuberance of the religion of Hindustan' and its 'self-torturing asceticism' (1973: 488). He postulated an 'undignified, stagnatory, and vegetative life (and) the wild, aimless, unbounded forces of destruction'. Even 'murder itself (was) a religious rite in India' (Marx: 492). For Marx, British imperialism in India, and its railways in particular, were a blessing in disguise. 'Modern industry, resulting from the railway system, will dissolve the hereditary division of labour, upon which rests the Indian castes, those decisive impediments to Indian progress and Indian power' (Marx: 497). Weber was of the same opinion. He asserted that 'modern industrial capitalism, in particular the factory, made its entry into India under the British administration and with direct and strong incentives'. He also believed that Indian factory labour lacked '(D)iscipline in the European sense' (Gerth and Mills: 414).

The modernizers' and Marxists' assumption of Western hegemony was the second similarity between the two approaches. The modernizers almost took for granted Western global dominance. They postulated an inescapable evolution from an undefined tradition to social-economic modernity, meaning Western societies characterized by highly industrialized capitalism. Industrialization was thought to be the main vehicle to universal social uniformity. Marxian scholars, or radical intellectuals, perceived Western hegemony differently: they saw Western dominance as a historically developed structural condition. Frank, for instance, expressed this dominance by distinguishing metropoles and satellites. Wallerstein demonstrated a European world economy with core countries and a periphery, and a division of labour between core and periphery.

Although they had different ideological messages, the global political mission of modernizers and Marxists was also similar. The modernizers were pro-capitalist. For example, Levy's book *Modernization and Structure of Societies* (1966) provided a 'setting for International Affairs' and was intended for 'graduate students resolved on professional careers in public and international affairs' (1966: 3). Rostow's popular book on the five stages of economic growth was written as a 'non-communist manifesto' (1960: 1).

Marxists and other radicals occupied an anti- or non-capitalist position, providing theoretical legitimization of social movements and political actions. Their analysis of the controversial historical role of national bourgeoisies, and the consequences of that historical role for contemporary national or international political alliances is a case in point.

Moreover, both modernizers and Marxists also honoured the ideology of scientific and technical progress. They shared a high modernist ideology (Scott, 1998: 4), which includes a faith in social engineering and in the possibilities of planning human settlement and production. High modernist ideology is, in Scott's words, politically promiscuous.

Last but not the least, they both regarded British industrial experience as the starting point and academic norm. Roots based his five stages of economic growth on studies of the development of the British economy in the nineteenth century. McClelland developed his achievement theory after correlating English popular literature from 1500 to 1800 with coal shipments to London. The Marxist-inspired discussion on the transition from feudalism to capitalism largely centred around Dobb's work on the rise of capitalist industry in England. In his illuminating essay, *Asian Capitalists in the European Mirror*, Mario Rutten (1994: 47) shows that the accepted ideas about British industrial entrepreneurs in the economic transformation between 1780 and 1830 must be modified. Historic studies show that the image of a class of courageous, adventurous, progressive, efficient, and able organizers needs revision. The proportion of merchants must have been considerable among this group. '(D)iversification of economic interests was not restricted to the upper class among the industrialists,' and there 'was a widespread practice of running two or three distinct businesses concurrently' (Rutten: 34–5).

Reading the empirical material collected by others also contributed to revisions to my point of view. These studies included Breman's work (1978) on the crushing of cane and labour by the sugar factories of Bardoli, Holström's book (1984) about industries and inequality, and Rutten's findings during his stay in central Gujarat (1986). Capitalist industrialization was a permanent feature in Gujarat. My visit to Bulsar in 1991 confirmed the information in these books. Industrialization, although still on a modest scale, was continuing. Several of the industrial firms I had visited in the 1970s had disappeared, others had prospered, and some had recently been established.

A few years later, Dale (1994), Goody (1996) and Frank (1998) supported my hesitations about Western perspectives on Asia. Goody (1996: 9) noted that '(t)he reasons for achievements in both West and East are more contingent. That leaves many questions to be asked and answered in a more particular, less ethnocentric way than has often been the case.' He argues to look at a wider 'span of world history than that from 1600 to the present day' (Goody: 9).

Homo sapiens appeared on earth some 100,000 to 200,000 years ago. The first major revolution in human history, the control of fire by primates, seems to have preceded modern man's advent (Spier, 1999: 81). The second major human revolution, the transformation from gathering and hunting to agriculture, occurred at least 8,000 to 10,000 years ago.[14] Many millennia elapsed between these two revolutions and 1850–1900, the period in which the Industrial Revolution started. This makes us realize that the period of industrial transformation has just set in. Capitalist industrialization has spread from the North Atlantic nations across the world at an unprecedented pace, but it has spread unevenly, leaving behind great social and economic inequalities among and within societies.

The 60 years between the first decades of industrialization in England around 1790 and the start of the first cotton factory in Mumbai in 1854 are, from the point of view of human history, negligible. Britain's lead of 60 years and subsequent political and economic subjugation of India by Great Britain certainly do not warrant conclusions that the people in the East, or rather Indians, are culturally, socially or psychologically unfit for capitalist growth.[15]

Politico-economic factors must account for initial differences and later economic divergences. Among these factors are contending European states and the consequent improvements in military techniques and economic assets (Spier, 1999: 133), as well as the subsequent political and economic imperialism. In addition, 'Europe's still productive backwardness (at) the turn of the eighteenth century have offered some of the 'advantages' to catch up. Europe's backwardness incentivated and its supply of American money permitted Europeans to pursue micro- and macro-economic advantages, which were to be had from increased European participation in the expanding Asian economies from 1500 to 1800' (Frank, 1998: 24). Dale brings back the State into the equation. The critical difference was one of political organization. In the case of the diaspora the defining contrast was the political fragility of the early modern Islamic empires, especially Mughal India and Safavid Iran (Dale, 1994: 137).

Doubts about the ethos, methods, and organization of South Asian businessmen have been Western-centred. The investigations to gauge opportunities for capitalist industrialization in the region have been unnecessary.

Yet, traders and industrialists do deserve scholarly attention, but as part of local, national, or international elites residing in capitals, towns, or in rural areas. The analyses of why and how certain groups are able exert power and influence, appropriate scarce resources, control labour, and how politics, government, and economics intertwine lend elite studies their importance. Methodological difficulties explain the comparative infrequency of the genre, inaccessibility of informants, like administrators, politicians, prominent businesspeople, and, sometimes, military staff, is one of the problems. Introductions by members of organizations and clubs, such as the Chamber of Commerce, Rotary and Lions, might ease the problem. The type of subjects to be discussed also might facilitate the fieldwork. For instance, informants consider 'family and kinship' a harmless topic, but it might pay the fieldworker. It can disclose that within one family there are traders; industrialists; politicians, sometimes belonging to rival political parties; and government servants (Streefkerk, 1981; Kumar and Streefkerk, 1985).

The approach of elite studies, why and how certain groups control scarce resources and labour, shaped the current study. After giving a brief overview of historical developments in Bulsar town and its environs in Chapter 1, I discuss in Chapter 2 the working conditions and labour relations in the small-scale industries in south Gujarat in the 1970s. This is followed by an account of the entrepreneurial behaviour of the owners of these small-scale enterprises. . . . In the late 1980s and early 1990s I was forced to reconsider entrepreneurial tendencies I had identified in the 1970s. My original bias towards Indian entrepreneurs and how I began to understand what happened in Bulsar between 1971 and 1991 are discussed in Chapter 3.

Elsewhere, I distinguish long-term and short-term continuities in the transition from pre-machine manufacture to capitalist industry in south Gujarat. Long-term continuities refer to the prominence of Jain and Vaishnava Banias from at least the sixteenth century and the emergence of manufacturing industry to the present day (Streefkerk, 1997). The short-term continuities pertain to groups that became involved in industrial production during the twentieth century. They have been, and some still are, petty producers. In Bulsar, local artisans were the first to change to manufacturing. The fate of one such group of petty producers, the Suthars, I discuss in Chapter 4. The chapter details how the Suthars, who started the town's first industrial workshops and factories, have fared between 1970 and 1990.

The past and present of industrial workers, or rather worker-peasants, of Bulsar region occupy most of the pages of the book. They work in unregistered and registered small-scale, or medium-sized industrial enterprises which are located along roads in the rural areas of south Gujarat or at GIDC[16] industrial estates in the region.

Rural industrial workers constitute the rural non-agricultural labour force. Its share in the rural workforce increased between 1961 and 1988. Kapadia (1999: 331) writes about a 'massive expansion' of rural non-agricultural employment. Forty per cent of all new non-farm jobs during the 1980s was created in rural areas (Unni, 1998: A-38). Manufacturing was among the biggest generators of non-farm employment between 1971–81. Mineral, metal, and chemical based industries dominated manufacturing. Industries based on organic materials such as leather, cotton textiles, food and metal products declined (Unni, 1998). In 1993–4, the proportion of men in the rural non-agricultural workforce continued to rise. The female share declined, though manufacturing showed more growth prospects for women in rural off-farm employment than, for example, construction or mining-quarrying (Unni). Between 1977 and 2000 the proportion of off-farm employment in the rural labour force grew from 17 per cent to 24 per cent (Radhakrishna, 2002: 247). The rise of rural non-agricultural employment has been caused by increasing casual employment (Unni: A-37).[17] Manufacturing, trade, hotels and restaurants, and services generated most employment in the non-farm sector between 1971 and 1988 (Unni, A-38); probably these segments contributed most to the rise of casual employment in the rural off-farm sector.

Data on small-scale industrial (SSI) sector show an impressive growth during the 1970s and 1980s. These data should be handled with caution because SSI units had been shifted in this period from 'medium-scale to small-scale' due to changes in the definition of 'small-scale industry' and because many enterprises are 'paper' units (Pradhan and Saluja, 1998: 1268–9).

Rural capitalists contributed to the growth of rural non-farm employment or rural industrialization, in the first place. Mario Rutten (1991) and Carol Upadhyay (1988) show how in central Gujarat and coastal Andhra Pradesh capitalist farmers invest part of their surplus in industrial production.

Second, urban businessmen and their elaborate subcontracting relations with rural producers also add to the rise of off-farm employment. Kapadia (1999: 342), for instance, describes changes in synthetic gem-cutting in rural Tamil Nadu in the 1990s. She argues that the proportion of women workers in the labour force rose in this sector during the 1990s.

Non-resident Indians (NRI) who invest in industries in India[18] are the third contributors. For example, Anavils who reside in the USA started a medium-sized pharmaceutical plant in the region in 1995. A family member managed the enterprise. Anavils used to be landlords and their children are well-educated. Among them are professionals, businessmen, building contractors, administrators, prominent politicians[19] and migrants to the USA.

Fourth, metropolitan businessmen who shifted their industrial enterprises from congested cities to small towns and rural areas where they found cheaper and more compliant workers, contributed substantially to the creation of rural industrial jobs too. The first batch of Gujarati businessmen from Mumbai, *Bombaywalas*, arrived in the small town of Bulsar, headquarters of the district with the same name in south Gujarat, between 1965 and 1970 (Streefkerk, 1985: 53, 54). They settled in the south Gujarat section of the extension from 'Delhi through Haryana, Rajasthan, and Gujarat all the way to the coast, viz. Ahmedabad and Surat' and Mumbai. Unni (1998: A-38) calls this zone the most conspicuous of 'long geographical corridors linking urban conglomerations'. In this case the links between the urban conglomerations are the National Highway (NH) 8 and railway between Mumbai and New Delhi.

The fifth contributor to rural industrialization and employment is the State. For example, the Gujarat administration emphasized the policy of attracting industrial investments to less developed rural areas through industrial estates constructed and run by the GIDC.[20] The Vapi GIDC industrial estate exemplifies the combination of metropolitan businessmen and the state contributing to rural industrialization:

> The Gujarati town of Vapi, on the border between Gujarat and Maharastra, is the last stop in Gujarat on the railroad connecting Mumbai with cities like Surat, Baroda and New Delhi.
>
> Vapi, which used to be a small and unimportant rural town is located at 170 km's north of Mumbai. It gives its name to the largest GIDC industrial estate in rural Gujarat. The estate, constructed between 1969 and 1972, is located at two km's east of the railway station, along NH8.
>
> Round 1993 the estate's ca. 1700 small-, and medium-sized industrial enterprises employed a total of app. 125,000 workers.
>
> Mumbai businessmen were 'pioneers' at the estate after 1975. They maintained that the initiative to construct estates at Vapi and neighboring Umbergoan had been taken by Gujarati businessmen from Mumbai. Conversations with government administrators revealed that wishes of the business community determined official decisions. (Streefkerk, 1985: 57)
>
> Relatives and friends from Mumbai followed the pioneers in the 1980s. Smaller entrepreneurs like artisans from Gujarati cities such as Surat, Baroda and Ahmadabad also settled at the industrial estate in the 1980s and 1990s. (Gorter, 1994)

Vijaj (1999) describes a small industrial town[21] 30 km south of Hyderabad in Andhra Pradesh as if he had studied *Bombaywalas* and the town of Vapi. He writes: 'The industrialists have strategically located their industries in the rural areas close to the cities. . . . The 33 new industries have come into existance in neither the classical urban nor the rural pockets but in new townships.'

The rural industrial workforce at the start of rural industrialization in 1970 occupies chapter three. The majority of these worker-peasants resided in villages in Bulsar taluka. The town with the same name is located at 30 km north of the border between Maharashtra and Gujarat. The chapter documents working conditions and labour relations in emerging SSI enterprises in Bulsar taluka, or Bulsar region. It deals with the mode of labour control and explains why the workers' common place in industrial production does not automatically lead to a shared consciousness, to a 'class for itself'.

In 1998, I again studied the industrial workers in south Gujarat. I stayed in Piruwadi, a neighbourhood in the village Lalgam. The village is located in Bulsar taluka 5 km east of Bulsar. The NH 8 divides Lalgam into two parts. One part of the village, located east of NH8 and inhabited mainly by worker-peasants, is Piruwadi which was my residence and research base. Sugar cane farmers, like Anavils and Kolis,[22] reside in the western part of Lalgam.

I stayed in Piruwadi from August to November. I intended to study labour differently from the way I had in the 1970s. Apart from material aspects, I planned to investigate immaterial dimensions of industrial workers' lives, like their beliefs. Further, I wanted to know about female industrial labour and what happened with the workers I had met in 1974. At first, the local social reality hindered me from accomplishing these two things. Friends in the village disapproved of my contacts with former industrial workers for reasons of status and prestige. Moreover, the production and consumption of large quantities of home-made liquor caused men in the village to thwart my professional curiosity. Furthermore, women were afraid to talk with me because they thought I was somehow connected to company management. Being an aging field worker turned out to be an advantage. I was far more relaxed than when doing previous researches: I dared to improvise more, and did not wish to keep things under control'. My behaviour and interactions were more in accordance with local perceptions of time and social priorities. I had what some industrialists called 'bearing capacity', the quality needed to run a factory, they maintained. In the end I got what I wanted.

Chapters 5 and 6 tell about the workers I met in 1998. In Chapter 5 I discuss the increased share of casual labour and the feminization of the labour force between 1970 and 1998. The chapter supports Vijaj's thought about '(T)he casualisation and contractualisation of jobs' (Vijaj, 1999). However, it questions his idea that both phenomena should be explained by structural changes in the Indian economy, like economic liberalization in the last decade (Vijaj). In Chapter 6, I describe growing social and economic disparities among workers and why workers worship Sant Asaram Bapu.

NOTES

1. The study was part of the modernization project initiated by Dutch sociologists and anthropologists Jan Breman, Chris Baks, Enno Hommes and Klaas van der Veen in 1970. They carried out research in the rural areas of south Gujarat under the guidance of Professor W.F. Wertheim in the 1960s.

   Later, they changed their focus from local to regional level. A new project was initiated and between 1970 and 1972 a team of Indian and Dutch researchers, based in Bulsar, investigated social developments in south Gujarat. They covered a variety of fields and themes in order to trace and analyse processes of social change in the town and the surrounding area.

   The results of the Indo-Dutch research project have been compiled and published in Pillai and Baks (1979). Other publications based on research carried out between 1970 and 1972 include studies by Jan Breman (1985) on migration and rural labour, by Arni Streefkerk-Hubbeling (1976 and 1979) on inter-caste marriage, by Klaas van der Veen (1975) on the joint family, and by Hein Streefkerk (1985) on industrial transition in the region.
2. Bulsar district includes eight *talukas*; they are Bulsar, Gandevi, Chikhli, Navsari, Bansda, Dharampur, Pardi and Umbergoan.
3. See Breman (1979) on mangoes and changing rural labour relation in the villages of south Gujarat.
4. The idea of alienation enabled Marx to articulate his moral critique of modern, industrial society. He thought that property relations of capitalist society brought about the estrangement of the workers from their work, and from their social and psychological life.

   Durkheim used the concept of anomie to comment on emerging industrial society. He meant the condition in modern society characterized by the breakdown of social norms and values. (He distinguished a new form of suicide caused by anomie.)
5. In the 1850s, capitalist industrialization happened in Great Britain in Lancashire, Yorkshire and South Wales. In France industrialization occurred in Paris, *le departement Nord,* Lyons and St-Etienne, and the France-German border area of Alsace-Lorraine. In Germany it concentrated in the Ruhr, Saar and Berlin. In Belgium industrialization was found in the Sambre-Meuse basin.
6. In this manner Weber argued against Marxist historical materialism.
7. These authors include Geertz (1963), Hagen (1962), Hoselitz (1960), Levy (1966), McClelland (1961), Moore and Feldman (1960).
8. They were neither in the West. In the eighteenth and nineteenth centuries, Britain's . . . 'initial capital for industry was raised through connections of kinship, marriage, friendship and local acquaintance . . .' (Wolf, 1982: 272).
9. *Jatis* are the basic units of the caste system. They are endogamous large-scale groups. The minimal segments of descent-groups form residential

units in hamlets, villages, towns, or cities. Localized units of the descent group are dispersed over a region or regions (Kolenda, 1984: 8, 10).

10. Politics is to be understood here as interactions to secure or maintain control over resources.
11. Their diagnosis echoes Weber's beliefs about the inability of Indian traders and merchants to make the transition from unscrupulous profiteering, that is *pariah capitalism*, to *rational industrial capitalism* (Weber, 1958: 112).
12. In a later paper, Fox (1973) kept himself away from this evaluation and rejected the Western disdain for pre-industrial trade in India. He concluded his article with the observation that present-day Banias were certainly capable of organizing modern commercial and industrial undertakings.
13. The distortions in the perception and analysis of non-European societies that resemble the biases that Said discerns in Oriental studies. Essentialism, like Dumont's contrast between hierarchical Indian society versus egalitarian Western society, is part of such distortions.
14. Spier (1996: 98) writes that new data show that the transformation to agriculture probably occurred earlier. In Egypt archeological material suggest agriculture around 17,000 and 18,000 BC.
15. Bangalore computer industry, Indian ICT and Call Centres, again, prove the contrary (Rutten, 2003; van der Veer, 2003).
16. The Gujarat Industrial Development Corporation (GIDC) is a state organization which is responsible for the development of industrial estates.
17. This trend does not show an uninterrupted rise. The rural non-agricultural employment growth rate declined between 1987 and 1999: from 4.32 per cent between 1977–87 to 2.06 per cent between 1987–99 (Radhakrishna, 2002: 247).
18. This tendency is described by Johanna Lessinger (1992).
19. An Anavil from Bulsar district, Morarji Desai was an opponent of Indira Gandhi, the Prime Minister of India from 1977–80.
20. In 1971, GIDC's annual report mentioned that 'new, rapidly expanding growth points are developing on the southern border of the state at Vapi and Umbergoan in which industrialists desiring to be close to the Mumbai business complex are setting up factories' (GIDC, 1971: 3).
21. A town of about 8,000 inhabitants of which 5,000 residents are industrial workers.
22. In Bulsar district Kolis are a numerically important low-caste land-owning farmers.

CHAPTER 1

BULSAR TOWN AND ENVIRONS BETWEEN 1970 AND 2000

In 1971 more than 70 per cent of the population of Gujarat,[1] as well as Bulsar district, depended on agriculture, which was most productive in the district's fertile strip between the saline coastal region and the less fertile hilly, wooded eastern part. The important crops were rice, millet (*jowar*), cotton, and fruits such as mangoes and sapota (*chikus*). Agriculture in the district was not very capital-intensive, and only 8 per cent of the arable land was artificially irrigated; the rest depended on natural sources like ponds, wells, or monsoon rains (Schenk-Sandbergen and Schenk, 1979: 25).

The northern part of Bulsar district, including the sub-disticts Navsari and Gandevi, was known as the 'Garden of Gujarat'. It was more fertile and less poor than the southern part, which included the taluka of Bulsar. Commercialization and modernization of agriculture had proceeded there more than in the southern talukas. The talukas of Navsari and Gandevi were the best irrigated parts of Bulsar district.

Seventy per cent of the district's population owned five acres[2] or less of cultivable land; 30 per cent controlled one acre or less. The number of agricultural labourers in the district was considerable. Many of these small peasants and agricultural labourers were members of Scheduled Tribes and Castes.[3] Tribals[4] formed the bulk of the population in the least fertile eastern part of the district. In the western villages they were also well represented.

The majority of the district's non-tribal population consisted of Hindus. Among them the Anavil Brahmins in the south and the Kanbis in the north formed the dominant land-owning castes. Moreover, the Kolis, a numerically important lower caste, often owners of larger than average landholdings, occupied in many villages politically and economically strong positions. The district also accommodated many Muslims and Parsis.

The central actors in chapter three, workers in small-scale industries in Bulsar taluka, had either very little land or no land at all. In Bulsar taluka, with 223,000 inhabitants, 75 per cent of the landholdings were 5 acres or less, more than 40 per cent of the holdings were smaller than one acre (Schenk-Sandbergen and Schenk: 26). The principal crops were rice, wheat, grass, pulses, and mangoes. Only 4 per cent of the land was irrigated with waters from springs or rivers, while the remaining 96 per cent depended on the monsoon rains (Census 1971a: 32-113). In 1971, there were 17,650 cultivators in the taluka and 14,372 agricultural labourers. The labourers represented 22 per cent of the working population of the taluka. They added to the pressure on agrarian resources, for while cultivators were barely able to earn a sufficient yearly income, agricultural labourers found it even more difficult. They depended on seasonal labour in the brickyards or salt pans in Mumbai.

Adivasis (Scheduled Tribes) made up 40 per cent of the population of Bulsar taluka. Of these tribal peoples, Dhodias were the sub-district's pre-eminent small farmers. They considered themselves superior to the other Adivasis (Kuknas, Naikas and Dublas). Dublas were the main agricultural labourers of the taluka and district, because Untouchables (Harijans) comprised only 3 per cent of the population.

In Bulsar taluka, which included the town of Bulsar, fewer people (52 per cent) depended on agriculture than in the district as a whole. Non-agrarian sources of income were more important in the sub-district. For instance, the chemical complex of Atul-Atic employed 4,400 people, or 6 per cent of the working population of the taluka. A further 4 per cent of the working population (almost 2,500 workers) were engaged in small-scale industries. Moreover, since 1964, when Bulsar became district headquarters, it became home for many government offices and servants. There were also many domestic workers, both men and women, in the town and countryside of the taluka.

A QUIET PLACE

Bulsar had been a local trading centre and port for many years. It was less accessible than the other parts of south Gujarat (Breman, 1974: 27; Gokhale, 1979: 81, 184). The small town was a local trading centre and port, and its inhabitants too produced textiles.

In 1671 the Frenchman Abbe Carre described Bulsar as '(a) small town peopled with Parsees, Hindus and some Moors. It has fine manufactures of cotton and silk stuff. . . . We marched through a fine countryside, flat but covered with low thick brush wood. I passed a pleasant time here in shooting game, with which this part of country abounds, viz., peacocks, partridges, hares, gazelles, tigers and wild boars.'

The town served as a market for cotton and silk cloth. Bulsar Banias acted as brokers for the Dutch and English East India Companies in Surat (Gokhale, 1979: 81, 118). The town owed its importance to its location along a trade route that served the needs of passing caravans (Gopal: 151). It exported silk and cotton cloth produced by Parsis, who were the finest weavers in Gujarat (Gopal: 209). Despite European and Indian pirates in the Arabian Sea between Mumbai and Surat, Bulsar merchants also traded via sea routes. For instance, in 1669 it imported timber from Mumbai. The wood was probably destined for the English shipyards in Surat (Gopal: 101).

The town, with a population of 54,966 people in 1971 (Census 1971: 22), was still mainly a service and trading centre. It was an important market for timber, mangoes, and other agricultural products, and in addition, numerous firms specialized in the grass, rice, and wood trade. Street vending, small shops, and large stores dominated the narrow overcrowded streets in the old centre of the town, the bazaar. The merchandise traded there varied from used dentures and spectacles, a few onions, bananas, metal buckets, devotional cards, to an abundant display of foodstuffs, radios, and refrigerators. A municipal survey included: 157 barbershops, 102 *pan* and cigarette stalls, 155 grain merchants, 75 textile shops, 52 bicycle shops, 29 hardware shops, 24 bakeries, and 7 drugstores (Schenk-Sandbergen and Schenk: 35).

Hindus constituted the biggest concentration of the inhabitants of the town, belonging to many different castes. A great diversity of 'middle' castes predominated, including artisans like Suthars, Luhars, and Kumbhars (potters). In addition, there were Khatris (weavers) and Ranas (who used to be donkey drivers and rice porters, but in 1971 they were largely minor merchants of grain). The lowest groups included fishermen, Dheemer and Tandel and 'Untouchables' like Bhangi. High-caste people, like Anavil Brahmins and Banias, comprised the socio-economic and political leaders of the town, and occupied the majority of seats in the Municipal Council. Parsis, who were not Hindu, were also among the socio-economic and political leaders (Thakore: 291-2). Although they had seen better days, several Parsi families were still among the most powerful in Bulsar, and for many years the chairman of the Municipal Council had been a Parsi.[5]

More than 10 per cent of the town's residents were Muslim. Generally, these were among the socially and economically poorest inhabitants of the town. Among them were weavers, oil pressers, barbers, and drivers of horse-driven carriages, the main means of public transport, and butchers.

Some 20 per cent of the town's residents belonged to the Scheduled Tribes. These included Dhodias, Kuknas, Naikas, and Dublas, who lived along the banks of ponds (*talavs*) in the town and in hamlets on the outskirts. At best, they lived in mud huts built on a wooden frame, but for the most part their shelters were dilapidated and offered almost no protection against heavy monsoon rains. These areas lacked sanitary facilities, drinking water facilities, and electricity. Street lamps were the only sources of light at night.

The poorest inhabitants of the town were the lepers and those who resided near the bus station, the railway station, and in the open area near the modern open-air theatre built by the Rotary Club. They slept in the large pipes used in the construction of sewers, or under a few sheets of plastic, cardboard, or jute.

The older parts of the town reflected the caste divisions. It was possible to find a *Desaiwad*[6] where Anavil Brahmins stayed, *Baniawad*, *Parsiwad*, *Suthar chawl*, or *Luhar tekra*. Neighbourhoods of high-caste people, like Desaiwad or Baniawad were in the centre, and hence the oldest part of the town. Usually two- or three-storied grubby concrete buildings alternated with nicely worked, but badly repaired, traditional multistoried Bania and Parsi houses. The lavatories of these houses and the poor huts of the domestic servants and others were clustered in the backyards, adding to the shabbiness of the areas. Open gutters running along these yards and unpaved streets seemed to underline the decline of these parts of the town.

During the 1960s the town's population increased and the town expanded to the southeast. Clusters of modern flats and bungalows were built by cooperative housing societies. Residents included businessmen, contractors, government officials, physicians, and other self-employed professionals. Some of these housing societies were almost completely made up of Anavils and Banias. In the 1970s, Bulsar was no longer just a port town: from 1860, with the construction of the Baroda to Mumbai railroad, it had become an important railway centre.

In 1853, the British Governor-General in India, Dalhousie, presented the 'Railway Minute'. It addressed the central issue of routing the major trunk lines. It would become the blueprint that guided early railway development in India (Kerr: 26). The construction of the lines meant substantial investment of British capital, the transfer of Victorian railway technology, the presence of supervisory cadre of British engineers, and the mobilization of millions of Indian workers. 'The execution of the works . . . is generally undertaken by small contractors or middle men, who in many cases are shopkeepers'. (Kerr: 151)

It took hundreds of pages of material in 1859 to describe construction accidents on the lines which included the Mumbai, Baroda and Central India Railway (BB & CIR). Accidents were major killers and cripplers. Diseases like cholera malaria, small-pox, typhoid and pneumonia also caused an enormous loss of workers. (Kerr: 157, 159)

The BB & CIR started to build a line north from Surat into Gujarat and the city of Ahmedabad in 1855. Once the hopes for revitalizing Surat proved unrealistic, the BB & CIR obtained permission in 1859 to build southward from Surat along the coast to Bombay. (Kerr: 31)

All steam-driven trains that passed on this route stopped in Bulsar for water and coal. In 1900 a maintenance shop had been set up, which employed more than 1,000 people in 1971. The railways gave the otherwise quiet Bulsar its special stamp. It was especially during the arrivals and departures of local and express trains that the station area abounded with people and all types of transport. The shunting of steam locomotives and freight trains in the railway yard contributed to the constant activity. The railways led to the establishment of the railway colony during the British period. It was a well-made, spacious residential area with bungalows, gardens, and trees that had been constructed along the rail line to house English and Parsi employees of the railway company. In 1971 residents came from all over India, from Punjab, Goa and Bengal. The colony formed an enclave in the town, as the railways were known to care well for their personnel.

The town also became a traffic junction on the south-to-north two-lane NH 8 from Mumbai to Baroda, Ahmedabad, and, ultimately, to New Delhi. The highway was one of the few asphalt roads in the district, for most roads connecting the numerous villages in the district were unpaved and difficult to use during the monsoon. There was still not a great deal of motorized traffic in the town, however, for the streets were mainly used by pedestrians, cyclists, and two-wheeled horse-drawn carriages, the main public transport. The most serious traffic accident I saw involved a panic-stricken, runaway horse and the messy aftermath of confused but unscathed passengers crawling from beneath the remains of the overturned carriage.

A BOOMING TOWN

When I returned to Bulsar in 1990 and 1991,[7] I found a town difficult to recognize. Its skyline had changed drastically, with many new flats, numerous TV antennas, and eight multistoried buildings, each with 10 to 12 storeys built after 1985. The main streets were overcrowded with cars, scooters, motors and scooter-rickshaws, annoying pedestrians. In the centre, new markets and shopping centres had filled up former open spaces or replaced old buildings. The Kantibhai Desai Cricket Stadium and Sports Complex, named after a prominent Anavil who took the initiative to build them, occupied an area which used to be a large open marshy pond in the heart of the town. The outskirts of the town looked different too. Along the roads leading out of the town, residential quarters had come up. For instance, the first part of the erstwhile quiet road to the seaside village of Tithal had become the site of opulent bungalows, luxurious stores, small restaurants, government quarters and airconditioned offices of businessmen. The largest slum area of Bulsar was called Shapurji Nagar. It was in the reclaimed Dhobi Talav on another edge of the town. To the inhabitants of the neighbouring housing societies, the slum-dwellers were a permanent 'threat'. They believed that these people were criminals who should not allowed to live within the limits of the municipal area. Actually, the area was populated by labourers, servants, peons and sweepers, rickshaw drivers, migrants from UP or Kerala, and by families who were forced to vacate their hutments in order to allow the contractors to build new houses. The area also had lepers in the fringe; they had been there for more than 20 years.

The immediate rural environment of the town also changed. More land had been brought under cultivation while some former agricultural plots had been converted into 'non-agricultural' land. This happened, for instance, along the NH 8 and the two state highways connecting Bulsar with towns and villages east of it. Traffic on these roads had increased enormously: the two lanes of the NH 8 were too narrow for the columns of vans which drove along them day and night. Along these roads small-scale and medium-sized industries had come up; A cooperative sugar cane factory was one of them. It signified the importance of the introduction of canal irrigation and the related increase in the cultivation of sugar cane in Bulsar Taluka.

The Gundlav industrial estate run by the GIDC had expanded. After 1985, a second GIDC estate had been established opposite the first one, on the other side of the road. The two estates, 3 km to the east of Bulsar, also accommodated branch offices of major banks, a telephone exchange, GIDC offices and flats to house office personnel of industrial enterprises. On both sides of the road there were tea stalls, repair workshops, shops of traders selling foodstuff or spare parts, and the houses of people who collected and sold all kinds of industrial waste. A service station for tractors and a recently opened garage were the most sophisticated establishments along the road.

One still found the makeshift dwellings of migrant tribal labourers along these roads. They used to come to cut grass, to work during the harvest, or in other kinds of unskilled jobs, like the maintenance of roads. Now they were hired to cut sugar cane as well. To the south of the town, along the river Vanki, 'Vashier Valley' was under construction. This was a residential area on the banks of the river where 85 bungalows were to be built. The project had been undertaken by the two biggest estate developers of Bulsar. The sales prospectus pompously announced that it would be fully equipped with infrastructural facilities such as water supply, street lights and roads, and that there would be a 'beautiful children's park and a riverside hide-out for all age groups'. The prospectus finally pointed to the 'famous Tithal beach, the site for lovers of sun and surf'.

Statistics supported my observations. For instance, the number of telephone connections increased from 650 in 1970 and 1,550 in 1980, to almost 2,130 in 1990. This was a growth rate of 138 per cent between 1970-80, and of 37 per cent between 1980–90. The size and growth of the population is one of the most revealing figures. In 1971 the urban agglomeration of Bulsar, including four adjoining villages, had a population of almost 55,000 (Statistical Outline of Gujarat 1989-90: 76). In 1981 there were almost 73,000 inhabitants (ibid.: 18), which meant a decennial growth rate of 32.6 per cent. The growth rate of the Gujarat population was 27.7 per cent in the same period (ibid.: 1989-90: 5). In 1990 officials in Bulsar estimated the size of the town and a few neighbouring villages at about 120,000 people. Even a cautious guess of a 100,000 inhabitants meant a growth rate of 37 per cent between 1981 and 1990. This is much more than the estimated all-India rate of 20.5 per cent. (Statistical Outline of India 1989-90: 37)

The growth had been caused by both natural increase and immigration: Bulsar became more and more attractive to outsiders who came mainly from Mumbai. Labour was cheap and the prices of land and houses were still low compared to those in cities like Mumbai, Surat or Baroda. Furthermore, life in Bulsar was more comfortable and convenient. It was a small, pleasant town near the sea and could be reached easily by train. Houses and flats were bought as permanent residences or as second homes. The latter was the case in the seashore village of Tithal, where Jains from Mumbai owned flats. Most of the time the buildings were empty, except during some weekends and summer holidays. Bulsar's administrative importance also had brought people to the town. It was a district headquarters with a growing number of offices and civil servants.

The unusual growth of the population was one of the explanations for the increase in building construction in the 1980s. The boom really started after 1985: the first of the multistoried buildings was completed in 1986. The enormous increase in new buildings meant the growth in the number of building contractors and real-estate developers at the same time. In 1970 there were only four or five major contractors, while in 1990 there were almost forty. Another reason for the building boom was that investment in real estates became a lucrative means to employ black money. There had been a sharp rise in the prices of land and houses. In some cases the price of land, for instance in Tithal, increased 10 times in a few years.

Many newcomers from Mumbai were owners or managers of enterprises which had been brought to south Gujarat in recent years. They were located mostly in the huge GIDC industrial estate at Vapi,

25 km south of Bulsar towards the Maharashtra-Gujarat border. In 1990 there were almost 2,000 establishments, which was 10 times the number in 1970, when the estate was still under construction. The estate was meant primarily for chemical industries. Due to serious air and water pollution and inadequate facilities in the small town of Vapi, owners and managers prefered to stay in Bulsar.

The GIDC estate of Gundlav, meant for small-scale enterprises, was another area where outsiders could establish their factories. Chemical firms were no longer allowed at Gundlav because Vapi accommodated them and administrators wanted to keep the area clean. The second estate, opposite the original one, began in 1985 and now the two estates accommodate 183 establishments; in 1974 there were only 20.

The old and affluent inhabitants also contributed to the growth of the town. They built new houses on the land they owned in the old quarters of the town, like Baniawad, Parsiwad or Sutharwad. They demolished their old single- or two-storied houses and built blocks of flats with four to five stories. In 1990 they lived in these new flats, and rented out flats they did not occupy. In the old part of the town an apartment of three rooms fetched a rent of Rs. 1,000 per month. The same apartment, but located in a more peripheral part of the town, brought in a monthly rent of Rs. 1,200-1,500.

There was a spurt in all kinds of commercial and professional services and activities. Compared to 1974, there were, for instance, many more medical doctors and private hospitals offering specialized services. Another visible change in the town's life was in the proliferation of scooter-rickshaws. Though they certainly quickened public transport within and outside the town, they were far from convenient because the roads were bumpy and the springs were bad. Their exhaust fumes, noise and their drivers' unpredictable behaviour were permanent annoyance, even to local people. The latest novelty was to have the vehicle equipped with a cassette player and loudspeakers on both sides of the passengers' seat, like earphones. As soon as the driver turned the ignition key, film music almost blew the passenger out of his seat.

Rickshaws replaced the Muslim-owned horsecarts, which were the main means of public transport till 1976. Since 1975 the purchase of a rickshaw was facilitated by special bank loans. Many rickshaws were given on rent by the owners to drivers. Among the owners,

Muslims and Tandels (fishermen) predominated. The Tandels lived outside Bulsar in coastal villages like Kosamba. They earned money by carrying in their boats goods smuggled from the Arabian coast into India. Some of the other proprietors were government servants or employees of large private industrial firms. Officially their wives or relatives owned the three-wheelers. The drivers were Muslims, Tandels, Kolis and Dhodias. Several of them were graduates and a few had postgraduate degrees. Driving a three-wheeler is often a part-time activity, combined with another.

Because official records were far from reliable, it was difficult to trace the exact number of three-wheelers in Bulsar. The files of the self-appointed chairman of the Bulsar Town Autorikshaw Association were the best source. Around 1970 he was one of the first to own and drive a scooter-rickshaw in Bulsar. In 1990 he ran a shop selling scooter-rickshaw spares at the main rickshaw stand near the bus station. His books showed the impressive number of 2,860 rickshaws in Bulsar and adjoining villages in 1990. It was hard to believe that so many three-wheelers circulated on the roads of the town and nearby villages. Several rickshaw owners and drivers, however, mentioned the same number when asked for the number of rickshaws in the area. Even though the figure might not be correct, it indicates a trend. When the self-evident sharp proportional increase in rickshaws in the early 1970s was left out of consideration, then the largest increase in number of rickshaws was between 1985 and 1990. In those five years the number of vehicles increased from 1,186 to 2,862, or by 141 per cent, while between 1980 and 1985 the increase was 116 per cent. Their sharp increase after 1985 parallels the town's expansion in those years. The growing number of rickshaws during the last 10 years meant that more and more people in Bulsar were willing and able to pay at least two to three rupees, the minimum fare, to be driven from one place to another. It also indicated the emergence of a new transport culture, which meant that riders prefered to travel even short distances by mechanical means for prestigious reasons.

CLASS, POWER AND STATUS IN 1990

Material changes also indicate changes in the configuration of class. The social composition at the top of the economic stratification altered since the early 1970s. In 1971, the Parsis belonged to the economic elite of the town but in 1990 they lost their economic prominence, though several families were still very rich. Furthermore, the number of prosperous 'outsiders' increased.

Banias and Anavils continued to dominate the economic life of the town; they were the wealthiest businessmen, and the richest building contractors and estate developers. During a raid by officials of the income tax department in 1989, when black money worth of many crores of rupees was unearthed, the officials caught only Anavils and Banias. In the 1970s, the economic power of Anavils was largely based on timber trade and mango gardens. This changed during the 1980s. Timber trade declined due to the policy of the government to save the forests. The traders closed their firms and became financiers or building contractors.

Owners of mango gardens earned large amounts by selling their orchards. Anavils with gardens in the area of the NH 8 and state highways could sell their property because land was to be converted into non-agricultural land, meant for industrial development. Other Anavils sold their orchards to Kolis and even a few Dhodias. These people could buy the gardens because they earned considerable amounts by the sale of their own plots of land, the value of which increased due to their strategic location. The sale of their gardens enabled Anavils to further intensify their urban orientation. In the villages Kolis consolidated their economic position or took over the economic prominence of the Anavils. Their economic ascent was a consequence of the introduction of canal irrigation and the cultivation of sugar cane.

The people at the lowest rungs of the economic stratification, those who only had their poorly paid labour-power to survive, were still the same. They were former tribals like Naikas, Kuknas, Dhodias, Dublas, and migrant labourers from more interior areas of south Gujarat or Maharashtra, and other poor Hindus and Muslims. They earned a little by performing all kinds of irregular jobs, either as self-employed or as casual labourers. They were temporary and semi-permanent workers in small workshops, small- and medium-scale factories, domestic servants, or assistants and servants in shops, restaurants and hotels. Their labour had no legal protection and they were still dependent upon the whims of their customers and employers. They were the inhabitants of Shapurji Nagar, others resided in dwellings in the old part of the town. Some of their dwellings were hidden behind impressive bungalows or newly erected flats, where they were not sure they can stay much longer. The casual labourers in building construction had a temporary shelter in the buildings they worked on.

The material position of this large category probably improved. The official minimum daily wage went up from Rs. 3 to 4 in 1974 to Rs. 21 in 1990. But often people were paid less than Rs. 21 per day. There has also been an enormous rise in prices of basic necessities of life, like cooking oil, sugar, vegetables, textiles, energy, medical services, accommodation, public transport and so on. Those employed in building construction did profit most from the enormous expansion of construction activities. Their labour was in great demand and they were among those whose daily wages were said to exceed Rs. 21 per day.

Wide social and material differences between the people of Bulsar and the population of the district in 1970 made the Schenks describe the setting of the research area in 1970 in terms of 'polarity' (Schenk-Sandbergen and Schenk, 1979: 18). In 1990 this characterization was appropriate when the focus was on the extremes of the town's social and economic stratification. The description would conceal several important tendencies which occurred during the 1980s.

Some groups at the lower end of the stratification had been able to improve their material condition. The much debated official policy to 'reserve' places and appointments in education, government organizations and politics for Scheduled Castes and Scheduled Tribes had even instutionalized channels of upward mobility. Employment in banks and government offices offered salaries and secondary labour conditions, like loans and security schemes. The schemes compared favourably with the insecure and poorly paid work in the private sphere. Thus, for instance, the material situation of those untouchables permanently employed by the sanitation department of the town probably improved since 1974. Dhodias and other tribals also could profit from the special arrangements meant for them. Moreover, the material expansion of the town and the surrounding area provided opportunities for the younger generation. These opportunities included skilled or semi-skilled jobs in building construction, better-paid jobs in shops and stores in the new shopping centres, or in industrial concerns outside the town or in Vapi. Regular and more income of some of the children enabled parents and other family members to better their circumstances. Their physical and social resilience increased, they could improve their houses, buy a fan, bed, or gas-stove.

The emergence of a middle class was one of the most striking developments of the 1980s. It was a major feature of the class structure of Bulsar in 1990. This middle class was made up of managers, professionals, small-scale industrialists, small businessmen, shop owners, government personnel, employees of private firms, and so on. They populated the multistoried buildings, flats and residential quarters, and patronized the fashionable stores in the new shopping centres. They purchased goods made available through the liberalization of the economy in the 1980s, like motorcycles, scooters, cars, refrigerators, televisions and other consumer electronics (ODI 1989: 1, 2).

Changes in the distribution of power accompanied the rise of the middle class. For instance, the composition of the Municipal Council in 1990 showed a much larger proportion of 'middle groups', like Prajapati, Rana and Ganchi, than in 1971. In 1971 these groups occupied 8 per cent of the seats (Thakore, 1979: 291); in 1990 the percentage was 31. In 1971, Anavils, Banias and Parsis occupied the biggest concentration of seats in the Council. The largest single group of seats belonged to Parsis, and the president of Bulsar's Municipal Council was a Parsi (Thakore, 1979: 300). In 1990, these groups lost their numerical prominence, though a Parsi was still the Council's president. Also the Rotary Club, the pre-eminently elite organization of the town, was no longer ruled by Anavils and Banias. In 1990 representatives of middle groups, such as Prajapati and Suthar, were members of the club's executive committee.

Anavils and Parsis no longer dominated the Municipal Council, but they did represent Bulsar constituency in the Legislative Assembly of Gujarat state. In 1985 a Parsi from Bulsar was elected MLA (Member of the Legislative Assembly) on a ticket of the Congress party. He was a former chairman of the Municipal Council of the town. In the state Assembly elections in 1990, he was succeeded by an Anavil from Bulsar. The Anavil, who represented the BJP (Bharatiya Janata Party), defeated the Koli candidate of the Janata Dal and the Dhodia candidate of the Congress party. He may have won the elections because of the strong opposition against the Congress party, which suffered heavy losses in Gujarat and elsewhere in India during the elections in 1990. Yet, it remained significant that an Anavil became the BJP nominee for Bulsar constituency, and that he was able to mobilize more votes than the Koli candidate of the Janata Dal. Kolis were numerically dominant in the area and the Janata Dal was one of the ruling parties in the Centre at Delhi.

When describing features of the class and power structure of Bulsar, I referred to people who called themselves Anavil, Bania, Parsi, Suthar, Koli or Dhodia. They claimed supriority and ascribed inferiority. They founded claims and attributions on more than wealth and power; they judged lifestyles and rituals. They belonged to castes or communities, and the ritual position of their primordial group decided about their individual prestige and status. Caste, community, and family status in particular, remained their major sources of identification and frames of reference. These determined lifestyles, perceptions of others, and interaction among people and between groups.

A growing divergence between caste, class and power components of stratification had been an important tendency since Independence. Economic developments, occupational diversification and administrative measures caused the divergence. Administrative measures included franchise, land ceiling acts, and tenancy laws. The Mouliks (1989: 35) show the levelling of the landownership in Gujarat since the 1970s. They show the dwindling of upper-caste dominance and the socio-economic progress of middle and lower castes and tribal groups. They explain this tendency by the Green Revolution technologies and the consequent socio-political pressures to enforce land reforms and ceiling acts. In south Gujarat too levelling tendencies and the growing discrepancy between caste, class and power could be observed. In the villages the political and economic importance of Kolis and Dhodias, who respectively were in the middle and at the lower end of the ritual order, increased since the 1970s.

In Bulsar, class, status and power still tended to coincide at both ends of the ritual hierarchy. Upper castes like Anavils and Banias were at the top. Their members were rich and influential in the political and administrative field. Tribal groups like Dublas, Kuknas and Naikas made up the lowest echelon of the hierarchy. In the villages they were landless labourers and owners of tiny plots of land and marginalized in every respect. They survived by circular migration, or by finding employment in cities and towns like Bulsar. Some of these migrants eventually developed roots in this new setting.

The prominence of Banias and Anavils was rooted in the past. Members of the two castes were merchants, moneylenders, landowners and better-placed government employees. They had a tradition of learning and monopolized higher education till the turn of the nineteenth century (Ghanshyam Shah, 1987). According to A.M. Shah (1989: 22) they were 'urban and rural-cum-urban castes'. Their members were the first to take advantage of new and lucrative opportunities in trade, industry, administration, professions and education during British rule and after 1947. Higher castes formed a larger proportion of the population in urban than in rural areas. Those castes with the least urban component were the last in taking advantage of such opportunities. Adivasis, who constituted the majority of the rural population in south Gujarat lacked an urban component in the past. The number of Dublas, Naikas and Kuknas in towns and cities increased during the last decades. But due to their social marginality and poverty, urban tribals were unable to offer lucrative opportunities to their rural brethren.

Middle and lower castes, 'urban castes' according to Shah (1989), abounded in the town. They were artisan and craftsmen castes such as Soni (goldsmith), Kansara (brazier), Bhavsar (weaver, dyer, printer), Khatri (cotton weavers), Hindu Ganchi (oil presser), Rana (rice ponders), *Darji* (tailor) or Mochi (cobbler) (Streefkerk, 1985: 22, 23; A.M. Shah, 1989: 9). Their members could improve their economic position because their original occupation enabled them to participate in the expanding and modernizing economy. Suthars became manufacturers of bobbins, contractors, or computer specialists. Ranas turned into owners of rice and pulse mills and well-to-do rice and grain merchants. Some Mochis owned shoe shops with large assortments of readymade shoes, including jogging shoes. Others, like Tandels, invested money earned by traditional activities, such as fishing and smuggling, in another direction. They bought rickshaws and became owners and drivers of rickshaws in and around Bulsar.

VAPI

The industrial heart of Bulsar district changed to the south during the 1980s and 1990s. It is located now at the small town of Vapi, on the Gujarat-Maharashtra border, 25 km south of Bulsar. In 1971 the Gujarat state started the construction of Vapi industrial estate. In 1994, the area, which is officially marked as a chemical zone, accommodated 1,700 small and large factories. This number made Vapi the largest estate in Gujarat. The biggest concentration of these enterprises were chemical industries (Gorter, 1994: 98).

According to estimates of the Vapi Industrial Association, these 1,700 enterprises employed 75,000 workers. This probably was a conservative estimate. Desai (1995) placed the number at 125,000, of which a minority belonged to surrounding villages. The bulk of the workers was from states all over India such as Maharashtra, Orissa, Uttar Pradesh, Kerala and even Nepal (Desai: 40). They lived in colonies located outside the estate, at its fringe, or inside the estate, where rents were higher. Others were given some shelter by the owners at the factory premises. Many had settled in surrounding villages, where their presence led to tensions between insiders and outsiders.

Living conditions in colonies are bad: Houses and rooms are small and badly built, and hygienic conditions are miserable: The absence of sewerage causes waterlogging, which breeds mosquitoes and thus malaria. Safe drinking water is scarce due to chemical contamination. Pollution of air by daily emission of all kinds of chemicals threatens people's health in yet another way. Living in Vapi is hard to imagine, let alone working for 10 to 12 hours in its chemical enterprises. Attempts to describe the stinking, steaming, and dirty collections of boilers, tubes, pipes, electrical wires and open drains wrong the harsh reality of unprotected workers. To a foreigner, used to state control over conditions of production, work, and living, Vapi is an inferno. Even those who are accustomed to it, however, do not take Vapi for granted. Workers do complain, but they cannot escape. Owners and managers who can afford to commute, spend their week-ends in Mumbai or reside in Bulsar. (Field notes)

In the 1990s the area was among the most chemically polluted regions in Gujarat. For instance, to travel from Bulsar to Vapi, several rivers are to be crossed. The changing colouring of their water, ranging from brown, red, blue, and purple, announces that Vapi is to be entered. It is commonly believed that birds flying over the water drop dead as soon as they reach the other side of the river. A fact is that in 1994 *sarpanch* (village heads) of about 50 villages in the neighbourhood of Vapi's industrial estate held a meeting to discuss the serious chemical pollution of their wells.

NOTES

1. In 1971 26 million people inhabited Gujarat, of which 1.5 million people lived in Bulsar district.
2. One acre is 4.047 m^2.
3. This is the official term for the socially and economically weak sections of Indian society who are to benefit from the official policy of protective discrimination. The policy reserves seats and posts for them in schools, colleges and all undertakings of the government and nationalized sector, and in state and central legislative bodies.

   MIf a particular region is inhabited mostly by those from Scheduled Castes or Scheduled Tribes, the representative for the State Legislative Assembly and Parliament must be someone from the scheduled part of the population. Bulsar is one such electoral district.
4. David Hardiman (2002: 176–7) writes that people who are called tribals now tended to be defined in nineteenth century vernacular languages as *junglijati* (wild community). Qualities like not following Brahmanical forms of worship, living outside the caste system and having their own ritual specialists, consituted their 'wildness'.

   The term junglawati was wrongly translated into the term 'jungle tribes'. In the twentieth century these people were given the bureaucratic label 'Scheduled Tribes'. In reaction to all this many of them claimed to be Adivasis (original inhabitants).
5. The real name of Freddy Mercury, the late frontman of the rockgroup Queen, was Bulsara. He was a Parsi whose family came from Bulsar.
6. The dominant section in the Anavil Brahmin caste use the surname *Desai* which has now almost become synonymous with the name of the caste.
7. In 1990 I stayed in Bulsar for three months. In 1991 I again spent three months in Bulsar.

CHAPTER 2

Workers in the 1970s: Discord and Compliance

This chapter explores workers in small-scale industries in south Gujarat, their working conditions, and labour relations in the 1970s. Workshops and small factories powered by fossil fuels and with investments in machinery and equipment of less than Rs. 750,000[1] were officially classified as modern small-scale industry. This industry was eligible for government support in areas such as accommodation, soft loans, procurement of scarce raw materials, and tax holidays.

In 1974, 143 small-scale industrial enterprises existed in Bulsar taluka. Most of these firms manufactured wooden bobbins, plastic products and chemicals. The other enterprises fabricated paints, rubber goods, or cardboard articles. These firms employed between 5 and 200 workers and represented, on paper at least, investments of less than Rs. 750,000 each. Many firms were located in or near Bulsar, a town of 54,000 inhabitants. The industrial estate of Gundlav accommodated 20 of these firms. The estate, planned and built by the Gujarat government, was named after the village of Gundlav, 5 km east of Bulsar. The estate had been completed in 1971.

The greatest increase in small-scale industrial firms situated in Bulsar town and taluka occurred after 1965. Prior to 1960 the industrial character of the town was chiefly set by artisans like Suthars. They had been the first in the town to manufacture industrial products, that is, the mass production of wooden bobbins. A transition from craft to industrial production began to occur after 1940. By the 1950s this

*The manuscript of this chapter was completed two years following my second round of fieldwork, interviewing workers and owners of small-scale industries in south Gujarat. The data used in this chapter was gathered in 1971 and 1974, and consisted of *qualitative* as well as *quantitative* data. Qualitative data was gathered from 53 workers during long interviews that usually took place over more than one session. A survey including 185 workers in 12 industrial workshops and small factories in the taluka of Bulsar in 1974 provided the quantitative material.

had already stagnated. Competition increased because more people established bobbin factories. Jain, or Vaishnava Banias, and Anavil Brahmins bore the post-1965 increase in small-scale industrial firms. Some moved to Bulsar from Bombay, most of them had been born in south Gujarat.

BACKGROUND

Until early 1970s most of the studies on industrial workers focussed on large industrial concerns. The leading role long assigned to this sector by planners, economists, and sociologists accounted for their interest in this 'organized', formal sector. Worker adaptation to modern industrial production occupied a central place in the sociology of Indian labour. Briefly, scholars and planners claimed that the primarily rural Indian worker remained rooted in a village culture, which led to large turnover in the labour force, high rates of absenteeism, and lower productivity.

The American scholar M.D. Morris (1960) was one of the first to criticize this view. Several Indian sociologists also assailed the notion that India's traditional institutions were barriers to the formation of a *committed industrial labour force* (Sharma, 1960, 1970, 1974; Sheth, 1967; Singh, 1973). They also viewed the idea of the undisciplined Indian worker as a myth. They showed that the high rates of absenteeism resulted from the recruiting and personnel policies of large concerns. Managers believed that these policies would keep employees in a temporary status as long as possible. The once dominant idea that Indian industrial workers hindered the development of industry has gradually and finally been refuted, although this is not true of sociology's one-sided interest in the workers of large industrial concerns.

Growing attention to the income generating capacities of the informal sector after 1971 led to more academic and official recognition for all types of non-agrarian forms of employment. Scholars included within the informal sector those jobs that were slightly or not at all organized, difficult to register, and subject to few or no regulations (Breman, 1976: 8). The informal sector, a concept especially relevant to the urban socio-economic system, was considered the polar opposite of the formal, organized sector. Changed notions about the Indian socio-economic system and ILO-instigated policy initiatives led to increased attention being paid to the informal sector. This sector was accorded government support and international development efforts because it compared favourably with the modern capital-intensive part of the industrial system as an income generator.

Along with the attention to the informal sector came official and scholarly recognition of 'unrecognized' sources of income. Nevertheless, intellectuals perceived the distinction between formal and informal sectors critically. For instance, Breman (1976: 9) argued that the distinction between the two sectors had to be considered a new variant of an old dualism theory. He noted that although this theory had changed over time, the underlying concept of a two-fold division had remained unaltered. The expanding modern capitalist segment opposed the slower developing rural one. Boeke (n.d.), the founder of the dualism theory, asserted that there was a clash between Western capitalism and pre-capitalist agrarian society. The former, he claimed, 'had been able neither to destroy nor to assimilate' the latter (Breman, 1976: 8). From 1945 onwards economists rejected this view. The modern urban industrial sector was now viewed as the motor for social and economic modernization and progress, replacing Boeke's ideas. In the 1970s the formal-informal distinction, as the most recent dualist opposition, constituted a theoretical reaction to the stagnation in socio-economic development in countries like India. The stagnation undermined the assumptions at the base of modernization theory. Breman maintained that '(t)he informal sector includes the mass of the working poor whose productivity is much lower than that of those working in the modern enclave; the latter however has no room for the mass of population' (1976: 9). Further, he argued that 'such a division concealed the unity and totality of the production system' (1976: 11). The informal sector, he asserted, was not distinguishable as a segment of the economy. Many large concerns could be considered part of the informal sector because, for instance, workers in large concerns were not protected by the labour regulations. Moreover, the practice of subcontracting integrated the small industrial enterprises in Bulsar into the formal sector. Thus, rather than segmentalization, a total industrial structure emerged. Social and economic subordination to large concerns marked the integration. Subcontracting enabled large companies to reduce labour expenses and to procure easily and with government assistance scarce or foreign raw materials and spare parts.

The concept of an informal sector offered little on which to base an analysis of labour relations in small-scale industries. Breman (1976: 12) correctly pointed out that this concept did not emphasize non-economic factors: at most it contained a few general references such as labour which, unlike workers in the informal sector, was supposed to be organized in labour unions, and impersonal labour relations.

The present research among workers, therefore, did not depart from the formal-informal distinction. But it assumed the importance of two variables in determining working conditions and labour relations. One was the general condition of a shortage in sources of income; the other was the local social configuration. These two assumptions will shortly be explored in greater depth. The 12 firms investigated represent the most important sources of both qualitative information and quantitative data in the research area. They included four companies producing plastics, two firms manufacturing wooden bobbins, two factories producing engineering products, two firms manufacturing chemicals, one firm making carton items, and one producing rubber products.

Two factors limited representativity. First, out of the 12 firms in the sample, 6 were located at some distance from Bulsar. These were four firms which were located at the Gundlav industrial estate 5 km to the east of Bulsar, and two factories located along the highway, about 10 km north of Bulsar. This is the reason why the survey probably over-represented workers coming from outlying villages. Second, the sample included two large and flourishing engineering plants which together employed 76 workers. They needed more skilled workers to operate complex machinery. They earned more compared to workers in small-scale industry in and around Bulsar.

USELESS FIGURES

The statistical data did not provide the total number of workers in small-industry in Bulsar taluka. Material was available only for the 70 companies subject to the Factories Act, but there were 143 small industrial companies in the research area. In addition, data were available for small-scale enterprises not subject to the Factories Act. Their owners wished to use government facilities. These data, recorded by the factories inspector in Bulsar, were, like the figures for factories, unreliable and tended to be on the low side. An incident that took place at the start of the research revealed why official statistical data was not trustworthy.

During the first phase of research to locate small industrial concerns within the research area, I asked one of the partners in a small plastics firm about the number of workers. The other partner sprang up from behind his desk and answered that he employed not more than 9 workers. The first partner interrupted saying I obviously did not work for the government. He told me that he employed 29 workers at that time. To avoid government interference, he added, he officially employed 9 workers.

It was usual for employers to admit employing fewer workers than they actually did. To economize on labour costs they kept the workforce as small as possible on paper.

The Factories Act, 1948 was the basis for labour legislation. The Act applied only to enterprises that used non-animal energy and employed 10 or more workers. The Act contained regulations covering hygiene and safety, set the number of obligatory paid holidays, and placed restraints on child labour. The definition of an industrial enterprise set forth in the Factories Act served as the basis for other labour laws, such as, for instance, the Payment of Bonus Act, 1965, which stipulated that profit-sharing had to be implemented in industrial concerns with 10 or more workers. Another threshold applied to companies with 50 or more workers. For such enterprises the Industrial Employment (Standing Orders) Act, 1946 contained detailed labour regulations. Moreover, these companies had to contribute to workers' retirement funds in accordance with the Employees' Provident Funds Act, 1946.

Owners kept the official number of workers low by, for instance, maintaining two sets of books: one for themselves and another adjusted set for government officials. Official inspections were confined to a routine few and, in any case, officials were generally in tune with the management. Another way to circumvent labour laws was to split an enterprise into a number of separate firms, each officially employing not more than 9 or 49 workers.

The data collected were no more accurate. Some bosses made it very clear that they did not appreciate my curiosity. To avoid not being able to see the workshop because of owners' opposition, I usually entered the firms through their workshop, at the side or back of the building. Then, on my way to the management's office, I counted the number of workers in the company: many workers meant counting less exactly.

I found about 2,500 workers in the small-scale industry in Bulsar taluka in 1974. At least a third of them resided in the agglomeration of Bulsar, i.e. the municipality and a few surrounding villages. The other two-thirds lived in villages scattered throughout Bulsar taluka and neighbouring talukas. I was unable to establish the extent my estimates differed from the actual number of workers employed in small-scale industrial companies in the taluka (Streefkerk 1985). The head of Bulsar District's Employment Exchange Office assumed that small-scale enterprises in the taluka in December 1973 employed 1,328 workers. However, he counted only workers in enterprises covered by the Factories Act. Moreover, many concerns did not cooperate because his count was based on data that was voluntarily provided.

The 1971 Census had little more to contribute since it did not count the workers in modern small-scale industry as a separate category. This census recorded 9,444 inhabitants in the taluka, with 14 per cent of its working population earning a living in industry, excluding building construction. This figure included an estimated 4,400 workers at Atul-Atic, the chemical plant on the taluka's southern border. How many of these 4,400 employees lived in the taluka was unknown. It was also unclear whether workers in Bulsar's railway yard were included in the census categories of 'transport' or 'industry'. Furthermore, many people from urban Bulsar and surrounding villages shuttled daily to work in factories in towns outside the taluka, like Bilimora, Navsari, and the city of Surat. All these made it impossible to estimate reliably the number of workers in modern small-scale industrial companies.

FACTORIES AND NON-FACTORIES[2]

The official underestimation of the number of workers in small-scale industry was typical of the state's marginal interest in labour. This problematic labour situation in workshops and factories was also reflected in my inability to obtain precise statistics. Moreover, the Factories Act, 1948 did not apply to many workers because they worked in non-factories. The Act certainly did not include workers in bobbin or engineering workshops, nor in small factories that manufactured plastics, textiles and chemicals. In the first type the actual number of workers was generally around 10. Small factories manufacturing plastics, textiles, or chemicals usually comprised several smaller firms, each employing fewer than 10 workers.

In one textile concern 40 people worked on 10 powerlooms. Several relatives living in a joint family owned the looms. The number of workers per loom never exceeded five persons. Another firm, with four plastic injectors, employed about 30 workers. They were divided on paper among three small companies: one served as the storage place of finished products, another stored cattle feed, a side-business. In the third enterprise a man made screenprints.

Non-factories located outside the municipality were not within any official control. Small companies within the municipality were subject to the Mumbai Shops and Establishments Act. This law regulated working conditions in urban establishments such as hotels, restaurants, movie theatres, commercial establishments, and also industrial workshops that did not fall within the Factories Act. It provided less detailed guidelines than the Factories Act for child and female labour, paid leaves, working hours, methods for paying wages, and rules for hygiene and safety in the workplace. Some of these guidelines were contained in short sections, and were less concrete: '. . . the premises of every establishment shall be ventilated in accordance with such standards and by such methods as may be prescribed' (Art. 40).

Judging from the situation that I, as a resident of Bulsar town, encountered in local stores, restaurants and such other places, I had to conclude that on the whole no particular set of standards and methods were maintained. Physical working conditions in small industrial companies in and around the town were equally bad. Workshops were poorly ventilated and the space between machines was minimal. Standards of safety and hygiene were low, washing and toilet facilities were absent.

Certainly, in hazardous industries like bobbins and chemicals, working conditions were poor and accidents often happened. There were many stories of bobbin workers whose hands and hair were caught in lathes. In chemical factories chemicals affected workers' skin and clothes. Management did not provide work clothes nor any other kind of protection.

Terms of employment in non-factories were poor as well. Hours of work and pay were irregular. Owners did not pay extra when production was speeded up and overtime was necessary. There were no paid holidays or bonuses, and employers rarely granted paid sick leaves. Management did not re-employ workers who returned after a period of illness. While it was true that on Diwali, which marks the end of the year, workers received a few kitchen utensils or other traditional gifts, employers had long been accustomed to giving such gifts to their subordinates on this occasion. In some cases, however, nothing was given. In one firm the Diwali gift was issued as a loan.

Physical conditions in factories were not as bad, because the greater number of rules seemed to lead to fewer abuses. Moreover, such firms were economically stronger. For example, two metal factories belonging to established companies with divisions and headquarters in Mumbai were more spacious and somewhat cleaner. But in these factories, too, there were unsafe departments. In one factory the final product had to be immersed by hand in a strong chemical. These conditions did not differ from those in smaller chemical factories.

Terms of employment for factory workers in temporary service did not differ from those in non-factories. Although the labour legislation did not distinguish between temporary and permanent workers, management and workers did. These terms did not appear in the Factories Act, Payment of Bonus Act, Minimum Wages Act, Employees' Provident Fund Act, or the Mumbai Shops and Establishments Act. Only the Industrial Employment (Standing Order) Act made that distinction. This Act applied to industries with more than 50 workers.

The Act did not apply to small-scale industries at the time of the research in 1974. It was in effect only for companies with more than 99 workers till 1974. During the course of 1974 the state reduced this limit to 50 or more workers, but it did not enforce the modification in Bulsar area.

Industrial employers invented the categories of temporary and permanent workers. They used provisions in individual labour laws as a basis for placing the workers outside the benefits of the labour regulations. The Factories Act stipulated that a worker must have worked for a period of 240 days during a single calendar year to be entitled to holiday pay. The same was stipulated by the Employees' Provident Fund Act: a worker could participate in this savings programme if he has worked a period of 240 days in a year. To be eligible for a bonus, a worker had to work for a minimum of 30 days. 'Apprentices' were ineligible for such profit-sharing. Owners called employees temporary workers when they did not satisfy these prerequisites. Among these 'temporary workers', however, there were labourers who had worked for the same firm for many years. Employers deliberately kept workers in temporary status by retrenching them after a few months on the job. Management replaced them by others or re-employed the retrenched workers after a few days. It also happened that owners changed the appointment date of the workers continuously without the workers themselves knowing it. Finally, management in companies consisting of more than one administrative firm transferred workers to the other firm regularly, either administratively or in reality.

Data about these procedures came from workers and employers alike, especially employers who complained of the shoddy practices of their colleagues. In one case the administration of an industrial firm employing about 50 workers simply closed after a strike in 1973. It proved that complaints were not simply allegations.

Registration of workers was done on small cards, as was officially required. The cards recorded, over a 24-month period, the number of days per month that a labourer had been present. After working for 240 days each worker was absent for a short time according to the cards. Following this break their monthly registration was continued for another 240 days. Then the card was almost full and a new card had to be prepared. The date of issue of the new card was thereafter used as the initial date of employment. Only these new cards were set apart for inspection by government officials.

Thus, for many labourers, working conditions did not differ much, whether they worked in small industrial firms, non-factories or factories, or informal or formal organizations. The survey data of 185 workers confirmed this observation. The majority (75 per cent) of the non-factory workers in the survey received no bonus and did not get paid holidays (79 per cent). These high percentages for non-factory workers are no surprise. What was unexpected, however, was the number of non-factory workers who received both benefits. It suggests the need of many of the owners of non-factories to employ some experienced or skilled workers and therefore grant them benefits and better wages.

Even more revealing was the number of factory workers without bonus and without paid holidays: 35 per cent received no bonus and 41 per cent no paid holidays. Of all workers surveyed 50 per cent received a bonus and 53 per cent no paid leave.

Scarcity of data made it impossible to determine representative conditions in Bulsar's small-scale industry. A few studies did provide information consistent with the situation in Bulsar; these included UNESCO studies carried out in Howrah near Kolkata, Ludhiana in the Punjab, and Rajkot in Gujarat (UNESCO, 1966).

The Howrah study (UNESCO, 1966: 59-62) mentioned the 'deplorable' working conditions. Labour laws were either not applied or largely circumvented. In Ludhiana's small companies the position of the bulk of workers was 'weak' (1966: 137).

In Rajkot (1966: 183) workers' conditions were miserable; small enterprises fell outside the purview of labour legislation. The researchers concluded that most of these enterprises were organized in such a way as to evade labour legislation.

An unsigned description of conditions in the small engineering industry in Maharashtra, particularly in Mumbai and Poona, agreed with the Bulsar findings. This description also confirmed the magnitude of workers' problems in small industry (Economic and Political Weekly, 1975).

> In Maharashtra's engineering industry about 100,000 workers fell outside the reach of labour legislation. Wages were low, working days longer than eight hours, paid holidays, bonus or other benefits did not exist. Small companies employed between 5 and 30 people, who worked under unsafe and unhygienic conditions. Workers lacked enough light, ventilation and space between the many machines in too small an area.

Thus, available information did not contradict the findings in Bulsar. Working conditions in and around Bulsar were more typical than exceptional for the situation in Indian small-scale industry in general.

THE LABOUR OFFICER AND FACTORIES INSPECTOR

Much of what factory owners did to keep down wages was an open secret. Their reticence to talk about it, and the attempts of some to prevent me from seeing the workshops were unnecessary. Their practices were known to those directly concerned and to government officials responsible for the implementation of labour legislation. This was also true for the owners' use of legislative loopholes to engage in illegal practices, fudged bookkeeping, and recording as temporary the status of long-term employees. In this respect, the distinction between factory and non-factory, formal and informal sector was deceptive too. By definition, government control over non-factories was marginal or completely lacking. Control over factories, although legally fixed, was also nominal.

In Gujarat, where the Department of Education and Labour was in-charge of enforcing labour legislation, the department head had his office in the capital Gandhinagar. The department had several subdivisions in district capitals and the important industrial regions of the state. Bulsar had a small branch office, headed by a labour officer. The officer defined his task as follows: 'Enforcement of labour legislation; listening to, and arbitrating complaints and conflicts between workers and employers.' The Department of Education and Labour also comprised the Inspectorate of Factories. Here the primary task was to enforce the Factories Act. Along with this the inspector supervised the implementation of the Payment of Minimum Wages Act. The Inspectorate had subdivisions in several districts. In Bulsar district the Factories Inspector had his office in the town of Navsari. The specific domains of the labour officer in Bulsar and those of the inspector in Navsari were not clearly demarcated.

The labour officer dealt with local labour problems and conflicts. This official knew all the labour laws thoroughly, but he did not apply the laws as well as he knew them. During our conversations he repeated the expression 'What can we do?' He further stressed that he kept aloof as much as possible from labour conflicts: 'Let them fight' was another phrase he often used. The real question, however, is whether he really remained impartial.

Although the employers did not have many complaints against him, the workers did. They called him indifferent. They alleged that he merely glanced through registration cards. 'When he first came, he made his rounds on a bicycle, now he comes on a scooter, and before long he'll be coming by car,' workers said. He was said to support the owners. When workers went to him with complaints about working conditions in a certain factory, he promised to look into it. But he subsequently spoke to the employer, giving him the names of activist workers so that the owner knew precisely whom he had to dismiss. When visiting workplaces to acquaint himself with the situation, it was said that he took information exclusively from employers and ignored workers. In 1973, a trade union, the Gundlav Kamdar Mandal, which has since been disbanded, brought up this problem in a letter to the Labour Commissioner in Gandhinagar:

> You are requested to check on whether a Labour Officer had visited Pearl Industries, and if so, whether he had met workers. According to our information a labour officer had visited the factory but he did not meet workers. He was only interested in speaking to the owner. When several workers asked the owner about the officer, the sheth (owner) told them that he was some representative of the government. We ask for your attention to this problem because in this way no one will listen to workers. We request you kindly to investigate the course of events. . . . (Field notes)

The factories inspector, too, had a poor reputation. He was allegedly on good terms with the employers. It was said that he would inform employers of his visits beforehand so that they could have the 'official' books available and 'superfluous' workers could be sent home for the day or afternoon. He too did not talk with workers during his visits. Once, a worker complained about conditions and wages, and he was promptly dismissed the next day.

Workers' discourses fitted in with the general picture, which consisted of employers generally opposed to research, officials with little interest in workers' poor working conditions, and evasions and violations of laws such as rules against child labour or against underpaid overtime.

The officials' partiality towards employers and their lack of interest in workers was largely a question of class. Income and lifestyle distinguished officials from workers. Officials shared the entrepreneurs' social position. Moreover, differences in caste status separated owners and officials from workers. Notions of high and low caste, superiority and inferiority determined how officials viewed their own roles with regard to the workers. From the perspective of officials and employers, tribals and Harijans were 'backward, indulging in drink, and idle'. Furthermore, owners and officials employed tribals or Harijans as domestic servants; the servants' servitude marked this relationship.

Workers perceived officials and employers to be 'high' castes. Most workers suffered low ritual status and no social prestige. Townspeople and villagers considered such work to be unclean. For workers, owners and officials formed one category, having common social backgrounds, lifestyles, and material positions. Social reality confirmed the workers' belief about the officials' partiality.

WAGES

Wages were even better criteria for appraising the labour situation in the small-scale industry than labour conditions or the enforcement of laws. Most of the tasks in small industries required unskilled labour. In the survey, only 7 per cent of workers performed skilled work. These workers received training in technical schools or in long apprenticeships elsewhere. Because of the agrarian background of workers and the unskilled nature of their jobs, employers used the daily wages of agricultural labourers as a guideline for paying newly hired workers. In south Gujarat in 1974 this rate was about Rs. 3 per day. One owner observed: 'Why should we pay them more than an agricultural labourer gets? At least in the factory they learn something and besides there is work all year round.' The survey showed that more than a quarter of the workers earned Rs. 3 or less per day in 1974; almost half of the 'survey workers' earned less than Rs. 4 per day.

Two engineering firms included in the survey used the largest number of skilled workers and paid the highest wages: Rs. 8 per day or more.

Usually, in the smaller plastics, bobbin, and chemical concerns, only one or two workers received such a wage. They were the most experienced workers who adjusted the machines and supervised the production process. They can be considered 'foremen'.

Almost one-third of 76 workers surveyed in the two engineering factories earned less than Rs. 4 per day. In contrast, of the total of 34 workers surveyed in four plastics and rubber companies, 76 per cent earned less than Rs. 4 per day. Only two workers earned more than Rs. 8 per day in these firms. On the whole, wages in small workshops, i.e. non-factories, differed from those in large companies, i.e. the factories.

Small-scale industrial workers in Bulsar town and taluka earned less than Rs. 5 per day: We will now see just how low such a wage was.

The Act specifying minimum wages in Gujarat applied only to a few branches of industry, such as the rice milling and bobbin industries (The Minimum Wages Act, 1948, with the Gujarat Wages Rules 1961). In 1969 the following minimum daily wages were set for the bobbin industry in non-urban areas, which included Bulsar and Bulsar taluka:

> Unskilled, Rs. 2.70; semi-skilled, Rs. 3.10 to Rs. 3.50; and skilled, Rs. 4.40 to Rs. 6.40 per day. The still older scale, dating from 1967, set the following for rice, grain, and oil mills: unskilled, Rs. 2.75; semi-skilled, Rs. 3.00; and skilled: Rs. 3.46 per day.

The minimum wages set for the bobbin industry corresponded to the wages most industrial workers in small companies received in 1974. They did not compare favourably, for the amount was a minimum fixed in 1969. Between 1969 and 1974 the cost of living increased enormously. In 1965 trade unions demanded a minimum wage of Rs. 150 per month, or Rs. 5.77 per day for unskilled workers (Schenk-Sandbergen, 1975: 199). Ten years later most of the workers in Bulsar's small-scale industry earned less than the minimum amount demanded by unions in 1965. The Third Central Pay Commission (1970–3), a government commission, calculated that the minimum wage in the organized sector should be Rs. 196 per month, or Rs. 7.53 per day.

> The Commission based its estimates on the dietary recommendations of the Indian Council of Medical Research Expert Group. It said that a worker required 2,800 calories daily. His family, consisting of wife and two children, together needed 5,400 calories. In the case of a vegetarian diet, the Expert Group recommended that it should contain grains, pulses, milk, sugar, oils, fats and fruits. (Subramanian, 1977: 318, 321)

Comparison of the wages paid in Bulsar with those proposed and suggested by the government and large unions confirmed 'officially' the low level of industrial wages paid in Bulsar taluka.

To assess the level of wages paid in small-scale industry in Bulsar we need to know what the necessary minimum should be. The Indian Council of Medical Research Expert Group recommended an intake of 2,800 calories per day, Dandekar and Rath (1971) considered 2,250 calories sufficient. Morris D. Morris (1976), however, found these estimates to be on the higher side, reflecting Western-ethnocentric bias. Even if a criterion could be set, it was difficult to get a complete picture of the various kinds of foodstuffs consumed daily or to calculate their cash values. It required time-consuming budget investigations, which could not be carried out. Instead other, more available indicators were used.

First, was considered external manifestations of poverty such as poor housing, bad clothing, and recurring illnesses like high fevers, tuberculosis, and other ailments resulting from poor health and an unbalanced or insufficient diet.

Second, wages were appraised by determining their purchasing power. In 1974 the price of the cheapest quality rice fluctuated between Rs. 3 and 3.25 per kg, *jowar* cost between Rs. 1.90 and 2.10 per kg, sugar Rs. 5 per kg, and cooking oil Rs. 9 to 10 per kg. Prices did not differ between the town and villages.

Consider a household consisting of an urban worker earning Rs. 4 per day, his wife, two sons and a daughter. If the man worked for 26 days per month, which was commonly not the case, then each month this household had an average disposable income of Rs. 3.46 per day.

A frequently used scale of consumption units assigned an adult male the value of 1, an adult woman 0.8, and children 0.5. Using the scale, this hypothetical household could afford the following food budget for each member respectively: Rs. 1.04, Rs. 0.83, and three times Rs. 0.53. In 1974 this could buy 346 gm, 270 gm, and three times 176 gm of rice per day.

These were substantial portions,[3] but one could not live on rice alone. This hypothetical household consumed considerably less rice in order to buy other necessary foodstuffs. In fact, taking other required items into account, it is unlikely that this household could afford rice at all.

When the price of rice was too high, people switched over to cheaper grains like *jowar*. In 1974 the price of the least expensive *jowar* was Rs. 1.90 per kg. Again, using the consumption units cited earlier, a disposable daily income of Rs. 3.46 offered the following possibilities: 547 gm per day for the man, 436 gm for his wife, and three times 278 gm of *jowar* per day for the children. This amount of *jowar* per person per day was considered sufficient, and other necessary foodstuffs could be purchased, admittedly in small amounts.

Continued existence demanded more than simply regular and relatively balanced nourishment. Money had to be spent on housing, clothing, medical expenses, and social responsibilities They included marriages, visits to and from kin, and religious functions. A disposable income of Rs. 3.46 per day in 1974 was less than sufficient to make ends meet: it was necessary to seek supplementary sources of income. The income of a household also included an industrial worker's extra earnings from odd jobs, such as helping in a store for Rs. 10 to 15 per month. A worker's wife and daughters often supplemented household income by working as domestic servants, and sons performed odd jobs in the bazaar or in restaurants. Such jobs provided about Rs. 10 per month for the wife, Rs. 5 per month and for the young girls and boys. Sometimes the mother would bring home some cooked rice or other foods from her employer's home during the afternoon.

These calculations are based on a household consisting of two adults and three children. Most households were larger and included more adults (grandparents and unmarried brothers and sisters). The contribution of an unmarried brother, if he had work, was usually higher than that of a woman from domestic work or from odd jobs by children. Thus, disposable income for large households obviously varied with the number of non-earning dependents.

Take a household consisting of a mother with a married oldest son employed in an industrial firm, his wife, their three young children, and two other unmarried sons. Of these two sons, one is unemployed and the other works in a small industrial enterprise where he, like his older brother, earned Rs. 4 per day. The average disposable income of this household amounted to Rs. 8.09 per day; it consisted of the income of the married son, his wife and three children as calculated above, plus the income of the younger brother. This amount, again using the consumption unit above, provided approximately the same amount of rice per person as in the first hypothetical family.

In large households, and certainly in those having several members who did not bring in any income, the total income was insufficient to pay for subsistence expenses. All respondent households were in debt. Most of these loans were taken to cover major expenses like home repairs, medical, or funeral expenses. Social costs (marriages and visits to relatives) entailed other expenses. Workers used some loans to repay debts to shopkeepers. They also owed their employers considerable rent-free amounts, and often these were withheld from wages as repayment. Many workers owed moneylenders and pawnshops; the interest on these was particularly high. Indebtedness meant even less disposable income.

Thus, a worker who earned Rs. 4 per day had less than Rs. 3.46 available, for he did not always work for 26 days in a month because employment in small-scale industry was irregular. Layoffs because of market fluctuations or specific 'personnel policies' were also responsible for keeping a worker from working the maximum of 26 days. Moreover, illness or social and family events also led to lost workdays. Last but not the least, workers often found out on pay day (which was once every two weeks or once a month) that they received less than expected. Employers deducted installments on loans and advances paid out during a work period. On pay day or the day after workers had to repay debts or pay interest to moneylenders and the still-outstanding debts to shopkeepers. Not much was left of the workers' wage within a few days of pay day, and it was again necessary to buy on credit till the next pay period.

A third method for judging wages was the workers' own views. People replied to the question 'Can you manage on the money you earn? with: 'Every month we are short; we have to go to moneylenders; my wife can't find any work now and we're absolutely broke.'

These calculations were based on urban workers and households. There are important qualifications to this sombre picture, however. In the survey, 50 per cent of the workers belonged to households owning a small piece of land; 90 per cent of this group had less than 3.5 acres, and 50 per cent had one acre or less. For these landholding workers, life was somewhat more secure than that of landless labourers living in Bulsar and surrounding villages.

According to the 1974 survey, the proportion of workers who lived and owned land in Bulsar was negligible (2 per cent). The qualitative part of the research led me to urban workers with a small piece of land in their native villages and cultivated by workers themselves during holidays or missed days, or by other family members. In one case, agricultural labourers were hired during the harvest for one or two days. The yield from such land served as a hedge against unfavourable times, for example, when food prices got too high, or during periods when little work was available and income dropped.

Soil quality was poor, and irrigation depended on the monsoon, yet most of the landowners (93 per cent) cultivated rice. Although most landowners produced for home consumption, a few households produced for the market. Families were never able to subsist from their land holdings alone. Rice harvested was considerably less than what would be needed for an entire year. Some families could carry on for a few months, others for more than half the year. But in combination with non-agricultural income sources such as their present jobs in the small-scale industry, these small plots of land provided villagers with some security. In addition, villagers obtained some income from vegetables grown after the rice season and from fishing, keeping chicken, goats, cows or, sometimes, a pair of bullocks. Urban or village-based landless industrial workers, who formed the other half of those interviewed, lacked this security.

Wages in small-scale industry were among the lowest in south Gujarat for unskilled labour. This was certainly true of the Rs. 4 per day or less that half of those surveyed earned in 1974. Agricultural workers and casual labourers earned somewhat more in the same year. Breman (1975: 28) noted that in 1971 casual labourers earned an average of Rs. 3 per day. He (1975: 19-20) referred to casual irregular work as *chhuta kam*, according to local usage. He noted that this designation referred to a specific type of work ranging from doing odd jobs on a daily or temporary basis to work of longer duration such as in building construction and road maintenance. Within this type Breman also included work done by sales help, clerks in small stores, waiters in restaurants and tea stalls, domestic servants, and temporary labourers in the transport and construction industries. He also considered temporary workers in small-scale industry as doing *chhuta kam*.

Uskilled workers in large industries, such as the Atul-Atic plant, received higher wages than unskilled workers employed in small companies. Also, municipal and state governments paid more for similar work. However, much of the work in these sectors was performed on an irregular and temporary basis. Moreover, it was possible to get around or evade the legislation regulating wages and working conditions. Thus, the labour situation and wages for temporary workers in these organized sectors did not differ from those of small-scale industry.

Compensation for increases in the cost of living was the important difference between the wages of 'permanent' workers in small-scale industry and similar workers in companies like Atul-Atic. Workers in Municipal and state governments were also eligible for such adjustments. In addition to the basic wage, workers in companies like Atul-Atic and government workers received a 'dearness (or cost of living) allowance' (DA). In Atul-Atic the DA was 90 per cent of the same received by workers in the chemical and textile industry in Ahmedabad and Mumbai. Workers in Atul-Atic received a DA equal to 90 per cent of Rs. 370 in 1974. A permanently employed unskilled worker in this industry, a 'helper' with the lowest basic wage of Rs. 31 per month in 1974, received Rs. 31 per month plus a DA of Rs. 333 which came to a daily wage of around Rs. 13.

In 1974, unskilled workers, 'cleaners' and helpers in the railway workshop in Bulsar earned, including a DA of Rs. 41, between Rs. 237 and 273 per month, or a daily wage of between Rs. 9 and 11. The poorest paid municipal workers, street sweepers and those who collected human waste received a basic wage of between Rs. 90 and Rs. 110 per month, which was supplemented by a DA of Rs. 107, giving a minimum daily wage of Rs. 6.57. A 'peon' in one of Bulsar's nationalized banks who had usually completed a few years of primary school and whose only task was 'to move papers from one desk to another' received at least Rs. 371 per month, or Rs. 13 per day in 1974. This was computed as follows: A basic wage of Rs. 117 per month supplemented by a DA equivalent to 220 per cent of the basic wage.

For all the examples cited above, secondary benefits were also better than in the small-scale industry. Workers could obtain loans at lower interest rates, free medical care and, in some firms and institutions, rent subsidies. These benefits looked better on paper than they actually were. Schenk-Sandbergen (1975) showed that there was poor enforcement of these benefits for street cleaners and human waste collectors.

Street sweepers and waste collectors earned more than workers in the small-scale industry. Nevertheless, the workers' socio-economic position was not as bad as that of sanitation workers. This group of Municipal personnel, made up of tribals and Harijans, depended exclusively on non-agricultural sources of income; moreover, they had very low social status.

Unskilled small-scale industrial workers were, indeed, among the poorest paid in south Gujarat: 46 per cent of the workers in the survey did not earn more than agricultural workers and other casual labourers; that is, Rs. 3 per day. Still, the financial position of most workers in the small-scale industry was somewhat better than that of casual or agricultural workers. Employment in small-scale industry was irregular and of short duration, but casual labour was even more irregular and short term.[4] Moreover, unlike other casual workers and agricultural labourers, among the industrial workers surveyed, many owned small plots of cultivable land.

A WORKING CLASS?

Workers in small-scale industry occupied a common place in industrial production, seemingly meeting an important material condition for a common social consciousness. While this might have prompted feelings of mutual solidarity, common interests, and formation of a social class,[5] unfortunately, many of the workers owned a small plot of land. This fact divided workers from one another more than their common position as wage labourers united them.

Along one of the roads leading out of Bulsar lived a family of which all the sons worked in different small chemical and plastics firms. I asked them about relations between workers and their readiness to undertake protest actions to increase their wages and to improve working conditions.

During one of the conversations, the eldest among them, the father, interrupted: 'Many workers come from villages such as Atgam, Ghadoi, and Khergam. They have land, they are willing to work for just about any wage. They are the informers and traitors during strikes, and when strikes occur, they are willing to settle for even lower wages.'

One of his sons, whom I met in 1998 (Chapter 7: 113), supported him by narrating about the plans to undertake an action in the chemical firm where he was employed. The acttion was meant to improve working conditions and to increase wages. Desai, one of the owners, who came to know about them, threatened to fire everybody unless they were willing to work for lower wages. Some workers, landowners according to Chagan, did not mind their pay. Activists were fired instantly. As proof of the bad working conditions, Chagan showed the mutilated skin of his hands.

This incident indicated that landless workers perceived contradictions between themselves and their landholding colleagues. The former believed that landholding workers were more satisfied with their wages.

When confronted with the landless workers' beliefs, landowning workers and employers had their own explanations. Workers with land found that it was difficult to stir the landless to action because they were too poor to take risks. Employers pointed out the same thing. They preferred landless workers because they believed that they worked harder to keep their most important source of income. They were perceived as less 'troublesome'. On the other hand, some employers preferred workers who owned some land because they were slower to complain about their wages since they were assured of a subsistence base. If landowning workers were more willing to work for a lower daily wage, however, this should be confirmed by a differential in wage levels between landowning and landless workers. The survey did not confirm this. What little difference there was pointed in the opposite direction: 46 per cent of landless workers earned less than Rs. 4 per day, while 41 per cent of landowning workers fell into the same group.

Landowning workers were also eager for higher wages. Although the economic position of small peasants was anything but comfortable, they invested a part of their meager income from industry into agricultural items. They hired water pumps and bought better seeds, fertilizers, or pesticides. A rise in industrial income could stabilize their agricultural subsistence base. It was impossible to conclude that the alleged reluctance to undertake and support protest actions rested exclusively on economic contradictions. Indeed, many workers, and certainly those without land, were neither inclined nor able to take risks. But a better understanding required more insight into the backgrounds of these two groups, especially the economic and social differences between the landless and landholding workers.

Those who owned some land had a certain economic choice that the landless workers earning the same wage lacked. The social component of this difference was even more important. Land provided prestige and entailed the possibility of making others, like agricultural labourers, subordinate.

The survey showed that landowning workers tended to have a higher educational level than landless workers. Indeed, illiteracy rates were twice as high among landless workers, and the proportion of workers who had attended a few grades of secondary school was nearly three times higher among those with land. This difference in educational level reflected a combination of economic and social differences between workers with and without land. It mirrored economic differences because more education implied a greater ability to pay the cost of education. It also indicated less need to involve young children in the struggle for survival. Social differences were reflected in enhanced chances to gain prestige and diminished the social isolation from illiteracy. Thus, a combination of social and economic differences and inequalities generated mutual distrust between landowning and landless industrial workers.

'Caste and community' made these differences comprehensible. Most of the workers interviewed were Kolis, Dhodias, Dublas, Naikas, or Harijans. All Kolis owned land and some of them possessed the largest tracts; many produced for the market. Dhodias formed the second largest group of landowners, but they owned smaller plots. The poorest in terms of land were Naikas, Dublas, and Harijans, who comprised one-quarter of the workers surveyed. The Naikas and Harijans who did own land, only had very small plots. The numbers of Kolis, Dhodias, Naikas, Dublas, and Harijans owning land were similar to that in south Gujarat. Kolis were considered Hindus. Dhodias, Dublas, and Naikas were called tribals and perceived to be inferior by the Hindus. Among tribals, Dublas and Naikas enjoyed the least prestige; the status of Harijans was even lower.

In general, Kolis were rated in the middle of the socio-economic scale. The survey showed that 16 per cent of them had secondary school education, whereas only 4 per cent of the tribals and Harijans had reached this educational level. The percentage of those entering secondary school but not completing it was 20 per cent among tribals and Harijans, while the corresponding figure for Kolis was 30 per cent. Some 8 per cent of Kolis had technical training, compared to none with such training in the other groups. Kolis claimed to have a higher ritual status than the tribals. They launched a process of Sanskritization[6] which was not disputed by others. They were among those who profited from expanding economic and political possibilities, and their position as landowners contributed to it. In many south Gujarat villages that did not contain any of the traditionally dominant landowning Anavil Brahmins, Kolis formed the most powerful group (Kapadia and Pillai, 1972: 42). Their numerical majority offered a second power base, allowing them to participate in expanding political and economic possibilities. In south Gujarat they formed the largest caste groups, which made their support during elections indispensable for competing political parties like Congress-O and Congress-R[7] in 1974. Besides, Kolis occupied important positions in local administrative bodies and schools.

The *Gazetteer of the Baroda State* (1923) described Dhodias as a 'primitive tribe enjoying higher social status than other "aboriginal tribes"'. This notion was still current in the district of Bulsar in 1974. Other tribes did not question their claim to superiority. Adoption of upper caste customs and lifestyles accompanied their claim. Along with other tribes and Harijans, Dhodias were the pre-eminent small peasants of south Gujarat. They constituted the local Scheduled Castes and Scheduled Tribes. Positive discriminatory measures and tenancy laws helped Dhodias to improve the quality of their economic existence considerably (Pillai, 1979: 327). Moreover, because of their numerical superiority, they had come to dominate the political lives of other Adivasis in many areas of the district.

Reserved electoral constituencies caused internal rivalry among the Adivasis. Dhodias used this conflict to their own advantage to get elected to the State Legislative Assembly and local bodies like the Taluka Panchayats and the District Panchayat (Pillai, 1979). They, too, had succeeded in occupying important rural posts in cooperatives, educational bodies, and similar areas. Thus, the economically and politically stronger Kolis generally had a higher status than the tribals and Harijans. This contrast corresponded with the social distinction between them. The landownership pattern further reflected differences in social ranking among tribals, and between tribals and Harijans. Politically and economically the more prominent Dhodias differed from other 'lower' tribals like Naikas and Dublas, and tribals as a whole differed from the Harijans.

It is possible to formulate a more accurate hypothesis about the contradictions that hampered mutual solidarity and promotion of common interests among industrial workers by taking these differences into account. The first clear difference was between Kolis and the tribals and Harijans. Better education and more social prestige helped the Kolis to occupy better paid and less insecure positions in the industrial companies. Tribals, including many Dhodias, received lower wages and were employed in temporary capacities.

Kolis got higher wages than tribals and Harijans: 41 per cent of the Kolis earned less than Rs. 4 per day; 59 per cent tribals and Harijans received less than Rs. 4 per day. Data on bonus and paid holidays showed the same pattern. Among Kolis, 56 per cent benefitted from bonus and 51 per cent from paid holidays; 31 per cent of the tribals and Harijans received bonus, and 25 per cent got paid leaves.

Thus, Kolis, because of their higher status among the workers, assumed a more conservative posture, which hindered the promotion of common interests. Later in this chapter this issue will be dealt with in relation to the strikes of 1972 and 1973.

The second contradiction was between the landholding Kolis and Dhodias and the landless tribals and Harijans. This contrast was defined in the differential ownership of the means and modes of production in the village. Many landowning industrial workers supplemented family labour by employing agricultural workers on their lands. This was true for about 30 per cent of the landowning industrial workers surveyed: about 21 per cent of the Kolis and 8 per cent of the Dhodias; none of the landholding Naikas, Dublas, or Harijans did this. The three latter groups, and some from the Dhodias, worked as agricultural labourers for those with more land. In the villages of south Gujarat these were mostly Anavil Brahmins. Where there were no Anavils, Kolis usually dominated politically and economically. Where both Anavils and Kolis were absent, Dhodias emerged as the dominant group. Relations between landowning and landless people in the villages also influenced relations among workers in industrial companies. The patterns of dependency and subordination in the villages reinforced social and economic differences among the various categories of workers in industrial enterprises.

Internal village configurations may also have influenced landless workers' beliefs about landholding workers' unwillingness to participate in actions to improve industrial wages. Such actions could go counter to their desires to keep down labour costs in the villages.

SUPPLY, RECRUITMENT, AND CONTROL

Ties between the employer and worker also determined class formation in the small-scale industry. Relations of dependency and subordination influenced contacts among workers and their ability to mount promotion of common interests. This will be clarified with the use of qualitative material. I started conversations with life histories. They were meant as a means of getting conversations off the ground and collecting background material. As many of informants had held more than one job, this method also provided material on how they found employment, recrüitment of labour, the nature of relations among workers, and between workers and employers.

Qualitative material showed that 21 of the 38 informants were employed in their second or third industrial job. Previous jobs had been in industrial work in Bulsar or elsewhere in south Gujarat. Eight had worked for longer or shorter periods in large cities like Mumbai or Ahmedabad. Nine had been dismissed from their last job or had been forced to stop working because the firms closed. The other 12 left their jobs because wages were too low, working conditions too poor or too demanding, or because the workplace was too far from home. The following examples are typical.

Case 1

A 24-year-old unmarried Dhodia, son of a postal worker, lived next to a pottery in Bulsar. His grandfather went from a village in south Gujarat to Bulsar. After completing a few years of secondary school the grandson went to work in the pottery. His job was to tend the ovens. He quit after a while because it was too hot and too difficult. After a short stretch of unemployment he turned up in a rubber factory which, too, was in his neighbourhood. Three of his young neighbours already worked there. They advised him to ask for work. After a year he was retrenched when he became ill.

Some time later he found work in a bobbin factory opposite his house, where he had been employed for two years at the time of my research. His daily pay was Rs. 3.25. About 12 labourers worked there. There was no bonus, nor paid holidays. At the time of my research, just before the Hindu New Year (Diwali), which was also the high season, he worked for about 12 hours per day; from 8.30 to 17.30 and from 20.00 to 23.00. On Saturdays his hours were 8.30 to 17.30 and 21.00 to 5.00 the following morning.

He was the main bread-winner in a household consisting of his mother who, as the widow of a postal worker, received a pension of Rs. 25 per month and who earned an additional Rs. 20 per month as a domestic servant; a younger sister brought in Rs. 10 per month, and an unemployed brother.

Case 2

A 26-year-old married Dubla stayed on the outskirts of Bulsar. His parents and grandparents also lived in Bulsar. After leaving primary school he was without work for some time. Eventually he found work in a bobbin factory. He soon quit the job because he continued to be hired on a non-permanent basis.

He was without a job for some time before getting work as a temporary railway worker, again through the introduction of a friend. His wife worked in the household of the manager of an engineering and typographical concern during this period. The manager occupied a floor in a modern apartment building near the Dubla's house. At one point he asked the Dubla, through his wife, to come and work in his factory.

The Dubla had worked in this firm for two years when I met him in 1974. From the start, he earned more than in his earlier work in the railways. In 1974 he was helper and paid Rs. 4.80 per day. He received neither bonus nor paid holidays. He was the main bread-winner in his household.

Case 3

A 30-year-old married Koli hailed from the small town of Gandevi in Bulsar district. He was trained as a lathe operator. His first employment was in a small factory in Bilimora not far from Gandevi.

In 1970 he responded to an advertisement in the *Gujarat Mitra*, a Gujarati daily, calling for skilled labourers to work in an engineering firm at Gundlav.

He was appointed and after working there for some time he played an important role in a strike in the firm in 1972. The owner closed the concern and returned to another enterprise he owned in Mumbai. The Koli and other workers became unemployed. Because of his role in the strike he could not find work in any other factory in Gundlav.

Through the help of a friend, who was his neighbour, he found a job in an engineering shop, several km south of Bulsar on the highway to Mumbai. The friend knew the firm's owner as the two had worked together in Atul-Atic for a short time.

In 1974 the Koli was employed in the engineering firm as a skilled worker on Rs. 200 per month, or about Rs. 7.60 per day. There were about 13 workers in the shop who received no bonus nor paid holidays. In spite of poor working conditions the Koli had no plans to actively involve himself in actions to improve labour conditions. He explicitly stated that any such action on his part would embarrass his friend vis-à-vis the owner and would thus endanger his friendship.

The three cases all show four methods for the supply and recruitment of labour: (i) a direct request for employment; (ii) obtaining workers from the immediate surroundings; (iii) recruitment through the mediation of third parties; and (iv) recruitment through advertisements.

The scarcity of gainful work and large supply of unskilled labour meant that offering and accepting jobs were perceived as similar to granting and receiving favours and obligations. In large companies and government organizations—the organized or formal sector—jobs were also considered as favours. Without *lagvag* (influence) it was difficult to obtain them (Hommes and Trivedi, 1979; van der Veen, 1979; Breman, 1979). Only when owners needed skilled or trained workers did they sometimes call upon the Labour Exchange Office in Bulsar. The same applied to the use of advertising. But even so, trained and skilled workers capable of operating plastic injection moulds or knew the techniques in the chemical industry were hired via personal contacts. Sometimes they came from the owner's establishment in Mumbai or his acquaintances there.

And there was always the *mukadam*, the labour broker. In western India he was called a *jobber*, who earned his living from recruiting and supplying labour. This made him somewhat different from those who did not engage in brokerage for monetary consideration. For instance, *mukadams* hired seasonal workers from rural areas for Gujarati brick works or Mumbai's salt pans.

In urban centres the *jobber* was a common figure. He was more than a recruiting agent. He also acted as a local overseer of the workers he enlisted. He came from the same region, village, or *jati*, as the labourers he mediated. Personal relations, employment, and advances given to seasonal labour during idle periods against wages to be earned gave him a powerful hold on the workers he enlisted. *Jobbers* were an important means of labour control for management of large factories (Myers and Kannappan, 1970: 97; Breman, 1975: 20).

In the workshops and small factories in Bulsar and Bulsar taluka, *mukadams* played little or no role because the labour supply outstripped demand: there was no need for the *mukadam* as a means of labour control.

RECRUITMENT AND CONTROL

The wide range of contacts between employers and the local population also made the *mukadams* unimportant as agents of labour control in Bulsar. In case 3 recruitment rested on ties between the employer, worker, and a mutual acquaintance. The mediation provided by a stall keeper at the entrance of Gundlav industrial estate exemplifies a more systematic form of brokerage. Although his actions were not a direct source of income, his contacts with local entrepreneurs enabled him clandestinely to connect his small grain flour mill to the electrical lines of the industrial estate. He knew about vacancies in local firms and recommended applicants to employers. Mediation by a third party was no less efficient as a means of labour control than the institutionalized hold of *mukadams* because workers felt obligated towards those who recommended them. Managers and owners used personal ties to keep workers in line.

Recruitment of workers via those already employed in the firm enabled the same mode of control; 22 of the 38 'qualitative' informants were hired in this manner. The group origin of the workers confirmed this mode. More workers from one village employed in the same company meant that they belonged to the same *jati*. For instance, five workers originated from a certain village, located about 6 km from the industrial estate of Gundlav; four of them were Harijans. Eight other workers lived in a nearby village; five of them were Kolis.

Van der Veen's migration study (1979) and another study of industrial workers in large factories (Sheth, 1967) corroborated group-based recruitment and supply of labour. Employers explicitly preferred this form recruitment and supply because:

> We are aware of new workers' backgrounds, we know the village or neighbourhood they come from, know their relatives and friends; they can't fool us. . . . We can always find out, for example, if they are really sick and, whenever necessary, we can contact them through their neighbours, friends or relatives.

Recruitment of workers from the owner's milieu offered the best opportunities of control. Eight of the 38 'qualitative' informants became industrial workers in this manner. They, or someone in their kin group, belonged to the personal domestic staff of their employer or his relatives. This mode included outsiders who had been accommodated on company premises. This happened, for instance, after employers brought their industrial firms and some experienced workers from Mumbai to Bulsar.

Industrial employment meant domestic work as well. Workers became part domestic staff, caring for the latter's house and garden, or working during important occasions like weddings and other rituals. For example, when the daughter of a prominent Anavil industrialist married, the Anavil put workers from his factory to work for three days doing small tasks including washing up the dishes used at the lavish wedding feast.

There was no clear distinction between recruitment of labour via a third party and from the owners' immediate social and geographical environs, which also made it impossible to distinguish different types of control for the various modes of recruitment. This was certainly true for workers of local origin, where owners enlisted workers without the mediation of others, though control was effected by means of third parties. The way an Anavil operated clarified this. His plastics firm was located on the Mumbai highway to the south of Bulsar, not far from his natal village, where Anavils were the dominant caste. Workers in his firm belonged to the same village. He remarked, without prompting, that he used others to control them. He referred to the parents, family members, and caste-fellows of his workers in the village. Another Anavil also spontaneously told me that he had a worker whose father had worked for his uncle. He had no problems with this worker because he simply informed the uncle whenever the worker was troublesome.

These relations exhibited features of patronage because employers admitted their obligation to offer such workers protection.

> You must help them when they are in trouble, and if you are going through a difficult period, they should stand by you as well. These workers are totally subordinate to their employers, and if necessary loyal to them. One worker said: 'What do you expect of me, I have held the Sheth (employer) in my arms when he was a baby.' This was the reason why he supported the management during a conflict in the factory.

These ties resembled the relations that had recently existed between landowners and agricultural workers in south Gujarat. They were founded on a debt the labourer owed to the landowner. Therefore, ties between owners and workers in the small industry looked familiar. Workers were provided with lifelong loans amounting to hundreds of rupees. Others received advances which had to be repaid in monthly installments and were subtracted from their wages. The precarious financial situation of the workers meant permanent indebtedness toward their employers. Major expenses like house repairs, marriages and ceremonies required these loans. The following case was one of the most extreme examples.

On a large piece of pasture land three separate firms belonging to the same family were built. Prior to their construction a few years earlier, a Rabari (shepherd) had been allowed to graze his flock on the land. The owner permitted the Rabari to continue to use the land even after the construction of the firms. As compensation, the Rabari served as watchman of the land and the building.

The Rabari's sons was to be married. The manufacturer gave him a loan of Rs. 5,000. The Rabari proposed that as repayment his three sons, already working in one of the firms, would continue to work without wages. This proposal was never realized, it was said, because his sons would not go along with it. They continued to work for the same low wages they had received and the Rabari began slowly to pay off the debt.

The manufacturer claimed that the sons are loyal because he kept their needs in mind. He asserted that if the Rabari had gone to a moneylender for his loan, he would have lost his herd long ago.

Employers stated that they gave loans in order to tie workers to the firm. This seems paradoxical when labour was so plentiful. But not all employers gave loans, and those who did went about it selectively. Owners guaranteed themselves of at least a few loyal workers by providing loans and other forms of assistance. Because owners feared that workers would leave once they had learned their tasks, loans also served to tie workers to their firms. Furthermore, loans might prevent a worker from being absent without notice for long periods. During such absences a worker would tend his own lands or bring in the harvest.

KEEP THEM UNDER YOUR THUMB

Employers in the Bulsar area were well satisfied with the labour situation in south Gujarat. The chairman of the Gundlav Industrial Association termed it 'tolerable' compared to the situation in Mumbai. He was overheard telling a Mumbai businessman interested in starting an enterprise in Gundlav: 'If you keep them under your thumb workers are not too troublesome.' Workers were less satisfied. They complained about their working conditions and the way in which they were treated. When I asked them why they did not do something about their working conditions, they often would say: 'This is very difficult because we are divided, we do not trust others, and we feel obligated to our bosses.'

The answers were on the mark. In addition to the internal stratification, dissension, and mutual distrust, the methods used for recruiting and offering labour were another source of discord and suspicion. They emphasized relations between employers and workers at the expense of a growing solidarity among workers.

Not all workers who owed their employers money, hailed from the employer's immediate environment, or were introduced by a third party. Nor did all feel equally in debt to those who introduced them, and not all equated the offer of a job with granting a favour. In every factory there were workers who acted independently. But each enterprise also employed workers who felt dependent and bound by obligation. Even when such workers were few, they hindered the formation of a united front.

Every firm had a Sheth's man, a *chamcha* (spoon), who kept employers abreast of workers' moods and fostered discord or broke strikes. Each workshop employed workers who had been brought in by other workers and who felt they had to obey. And every owner maintained relations with outsiders who guaranteed the loyalty of some workers to the concern.

Local social configurations reinforced the domination of employers over employees. Most of the owners belonged to twice-born[8] castes such as Anavil Brahmins or Banias, or castes that claimed such a status, such as Suthars. The workers were Kolis, Dhodias, Naikas, Dublas, or Harijans, who were considered socially inferior and described as 'backward' by the owners.

Differences in status and prestige had a material component. Anavils and Banias had long dominated the rural political-economic system. This dominance left an indelible stamp on their behaviour towards their subordinates. The latter still depended on them as small peasants, landless agricultural labourers, or as debtors. Anavils controlled access to scarce resources like land and jobs, and Banias were the age-old monetary source. Local hierarchical relations also accounted for the authoritarian behaviour of employers and the compliance of workers.

Owners exercised their power harshly. Workers were threatened with withdrawal of little benefits like toilet breaks, convenient hours of the workday, or with wage cuts. During a visit to a chemical concern, the Anavil owner confessed that he used to carry a stick with him while making rounds in the factory. He no longer did so because he was too old for it and could manage well enough without it. This he demonstrated a few moments later when he shouted in coarse language that two workers had done something wrong and how stupid they were.

The shortage of jobs empowered employers even further. Their command over jobs, a scarce resource, enabled them to bind workers and to put them 'into harness'. Their call on third parties to force workers to obey would be ineffective if it were not accompanied by threats of being sacked.

Dismissal was one of the most commonly used threats. Employers invoked it even on the first day of work. They made workers sign a statement in which they promised, on pain of being dismissed, not to join any union and to refrain from anti-work actions. The effectiveness of the sanction was apparent from workers' statements such as 'we are too poor to resist'. Obviously, workers could not afford to earn less or lose their jobs, thereby reducing the income of their households.

ACTIONS

Workers were part of a closed system of controls, and compliance and submissiveness fed by powerlessness seemed to be inevitable. Yet there were variations. Intimidation of workers and the need 'to keep them under the (employer's) thumb' showed that personal dependencies and differences among workers were not always effective. Owners had to reckon with less apathetic and less submissive workers, and they could not completely repress feelings of discord and non-compliance. Conversations with workers showed their feelings of annoyance and resentment. A series of strikes and actions during the late 1960s and in 1972 and 1973 proved that workers could be stirred. At issue were wage increases, an introduction of or increase in bonuses, and granting paid holidays and special rights to workers with many years of service in an enterprise.

By 1974, several actions had taken place in the research area: six will be discussed below. Other incidents lacked sufficient and consistent data, which hindered a proper reconstruction of these events.

The actions and strikes are significant because they indicate discontent among workers and expose the manner in which owners tried to suppress actions and control workers. Moreover, they reveal the participation of landowning workers in actions. And these actions provide insight into how local unions worked and their leadership.

The first strike (*Action A*) in Bulsar's small industry was said to have taken place in 1969. Fifteen workers of a rubber concern, whose headquarters was in Mumbai, went on strike, demanding higher wages, bonus and paid holidays, since the firm had shown a substantial profit the previous year. The strike was led by a landowning Dhodia. He had been in contact with the secretary of the INTUC[9]-affiliated

Bulsar District Industrial Employees' Union (BDIEU). The Dhodia acted as the firm's BDIEU representative, collected union dues, and discussed workers' demands with the BDIEU secretary. The secretary advised a strike; he assembled workers in a public park and called on them to strike for 14 days, but the action lasted only 4 or 5 days.

According to the Dhodia strike leader, the union secretary misled the workers. He had not told them that strikes were legal only if they were declared with 14 days' notice.

In any case, the firm's oldest employee, a Dubla, broke the strike. The owner's family employed his father; the son admitted that he could not possibly refuse the proprietor's orders. The owner visited the Dubla's house and together they went to an adjacent village to hire new workers. They were other Dublas (*jatibhaio*) who had previously worked for a short time in the firm. Production was restarted and the owner sent word through the Dubla to the striking workers that they would receive a raise of 0.25 paise (1 paisa = Rs. 0.01) per month and a 4 per cent bonus if they returned to work. If they did not call off the strike they would be dismissed. One by one the strikers reported back to work and after a few weeks the extra workers were laid off.

The Dhodia strike leader left the concern some time later. His departure ended labour organization among workers in the factory. The employer threatened to summarily dismiss any worker who tried to organize workers and anyone who joined a union. Permanent workers received the wage raise, but the owner did not pay the promised annual bonus between 1969 and 1973.

In 1974 the Dubla strike-breaker still worked in the enterprise against a wage of Rs. 5 per day. Other workers got a daily wage of Rs. 3 to 4. A technically experienced worker earned considerably more, Rs. 7.50 per day.

Initially, the colleagues did not like the Dubla's behaviour during the strike, but some of them understood his difficult position and the role which he was forced to play.

In 1974 the Dubla still acted as a go-between other workers and the employer. Co-workers who wanted something from the employer would go to the Dubla first, rather than directly to the employer, as he was not afraid to ask favours from the employer.

In early 1972, under the leadership of the BDIEU secretary, workers began to press demands in several factories located along the two roads leading east and south out of Bulsar (*Action B*). The secretary addressed workers at the end of the working day as they passed through the factory gates; he stressed their poor working conditions and low wages, and advised them to join the BDIEU. Workers responded to the call, and the secretary sent similar letters to several factory owners, charging them with breaking regulations of the Factories Act. He demanded the end of these offences and increase in wages. He threatened strikes if owners did not meet these demands. Copies of the letters were sent to the labour officer in Bulsar and the labour commissioner in Ahmedabad. The primary goal of the BDIEU official was to promote his own interests and to reach an agreement with owners quickly. Owners said that forging a compromise simply involved negotiating the BDIEU secretary's demands: the size of his bribe. In exchange for this the secretary was prepared to drop some of the demands and to moderate the requested wage increases. Unwilling employers had to face strikes.

The owner of an engineering factory with protesting workers (*Action B*) dismissed six temporary workers and, a few days later, the most active strikers. Other workers tried to negotiate; six days later they returned to work. In the meantime the BDIEU secretary had sent his demands to the labour officer and labour commissioner in Gandhinagar. The owner claimed the he could not afford to compromise since his factory had been operating at a loss during this period. The labour tribunal summoned both parties, the BDIEU represented by an INTUC lawyer and the owner, to Gandhinagar. The tribunal handed down a decision one and a half years later. It called for a small rise in wages and more paid holidays.

In another case (*Actions C* and *D*) the BDIEU secretary caused the owner of two plastics firms a few problems. The two companies were located near the engineering factory (mentioned earlier), and the strikes took place at the same time. The owner summarily dismissed striking workers. He offered workers who were willing to compromise, as well as those who were considering doing so, a wage rise of a few paise per day. The strike fizzled out after two days. Later, the labour tribunal in Ahmedabad ruled that the BDIEU demands were inapplicable to these two firms because they were not registered as factories. The firms employed 15 and 25 workers respectively.

During the same period, the fourth strike (*Action E*) occurred in a large metal-working enterprise employing about 80 to 90 workers.

The conflict began like *Actions B*, *C* and *D*. A compromise was quickly reached; management agreed to wage increases of 1 to 2 paisa per day, which would be repeated annually up to and including 1976. The agreement was approved by the labour commissioner in Ahmedabad, and the BDIEU dropped its action. A few months later another union organizer launched an action in the same factory. He was the secretary of the Samanya Karmachari Sangh (SKS). Until then he had been primarily involved in organizing municipal and government workers in and around Bulsar. He lived in Bulsar, and his union was affiliated with the Bhartiya Mazdoor Sangh (BMS), which maintained close ties with the rightist Hindu party, Jan Sangh. The SKS secretary stood up for a dismissed worker; as the reasons for the worker's dismissal were unclear, the BDIEU did not take up his cause. Moreover, the workers were dissatisfied with the compromise negotiated by the BDIEU secretary. Once the settlement was reached, the BDIEU official was indifferent to violations of regulations, even though the employer only minimally fulfilled his promises. The SKS leader drew up a long list of demands, including better treatment of temporary workers, more paid holidays and, most important, adjustment of the wage scale to the levels recommended by the Central Wage Board for Engineering Industries. He sent copies of his demands to the labour officer in Bulsar and the labour commissioner in Ahmedabad. The management rejected these demands and referred them back to the agreement reached with the BDIEU secretary. Subsequently, the SKS leader called for a strike, and the owner dismissed 82 employees.

The list of demands now included immediate reinstatement of the dismissed workers. The strike lasted several months. Apparently, the most important issue at stake was the implementation of the recommended wage levels for the entire engineering industry in south Gujarat and not just the firm directly involved. In September 1972 the strike ended. The management imported replacement workers with police escort. Moreover, many workers, except those whom the union had managed to shelter elsewhere, had long been without income and could therefore be easily persuaded to return to work. Using money supplied by the company, the rival BDIEU allegedly bought off the most active union workers while the SKS official was negotiating in Ahmedabad.

The remaining striking workers resumed work after they agreed to drop all demands in exchange for the promise that dismissed employees would be reinstated. This settlement was confirmed in a letter from the labour tribunal.

The SKS organizer once again managed to get workers in the same engineering factory to follow him because the BDIEU secretary had left for Surat. The dismissal of four workers who had taken part in the 1972 strike enabled the SKS organizer to act again. The unsettled question of the implementation of a minimum wage offered the SKS organizer the opportunity to demand implementation of the wage recommendations and again threaten a strike. Subsequently, the owner and SKS organizer reached an agreement in which the owner promised to adopt the wage levels recommended by the Engineering Wage Board from January 1974 onwards. The Labour Commissioner in Ahmedabad ratified the settlement, and damages were limited because the management could continue to set the wage levels. The SKS and its member-workers won a victory in principles.

Management based new wage scales on workers' skills about which management decided. Thus, in 1974, about 54 of the 83 workers were registered as unskilled, 24 as semi-skilled, and 5 as skilled.

The minimum wage in force after the settlement was Rs. 122 per month, or about Rs. 4.50 per day. It was a slight improvement over the previous pay and slightly better than the average wages paid to the 185 workers surveyed.[10]

Employees classified as temporary labourers were excluded from the settlement. By the third quarter of 1974, conditions of the settlement were not implemented.

The departure of the BDIEU leader led to the SKS secretary's victory because management could then come to terms with him by offering a slight wage increase and accepting the SKS secretary as mediator between management and workers. The success of the SKS had a political basis as well, for the union was linked to the Jan Sangh, which fervently opposed Indira Gandhi and her Congress-R. Industrial entrepreneurs and other south Gujarati businessmen were also opposed to Indira Gandhi and her party. The conciliatory attitude adopted by the management towards the SKS could be explained by their common political interests.

The sixth strike took place in an engineering firm at Gundlav. The company consisted of two separate enterprises manufacturing different products. The two firms together employed 40 to 50 workers who were kept in temporary status. Clashes (*Action F*) in this firm began in 1973. The prime mover behind the strike was a technically trained Koli.

The immediate cause of Koli's involvement was the dismissal of a senior worker. He had come from the firm's Mumbai division, where he had worked for many years. He was transferred to Gundlav to join the few skilled workers there. In spite of his many years of service in Mumbai, the Gundlav manager placed him on par with temporary workers. He protested and was dismissed on the spot. The Koli then realized how weak his own position was and resolved to do something about it.

The Koli discussed his plan with one of his colleagues and the Gundlav stall keeper. They founded the labour organization of Gundlav, the Gundlav Kamdar Mandal (GKM). To give the GKM formal status, the shopkeeper, a Congress-R supporter, approached the local Congress-R political candidate, who arranged for official recognition of the GKM and the appointment of a union leader who represented the INTUC. He also supported the Congress-R.

The owner reacted resolutely. He closed down the Gundlav firm and returned to Mumbai where he owned other enterprises. The firm's closing meant the end of the GKM. Other owners gleefully used the incident as a warning against worker actions. The most active GMK members disappeared, and the complaints lodged with the labour commissioner were not considered because they lacked active union support, and individual workers could not afford to cover the administrative costs.

The shopkeeper-cum-organizer dropped his union activities. 'Workers were too frightened and they would never get involved because they were too easily satisfied with their wages due to their landholdings.' He was also under pressure from the owners to keep his distance. He was told that if he continued his union activities his illegal electric supply would be cut off. 'You have to understand,' he said, 'that as a locally-based man, you can't get involved with this kind of an affair because you can end up in a lot of trouble.' At the time of the research, he was again on good terms with factory owners in the industrial estate. He managed to keep workers obliged to him by recommending them for jobs.

Two of these actions failed (*Actions C, D*), one was a pyrrhic victory (*Action F*), and three strikes (*Actions A, B, E*) were successful.

Wages were raised, a bonus was promised and occasionally paid, and striking workers were rehired. But the strikes were detrimental to temporary employees. Most of them were dismissed and never taken back. While benefits were given to the 'permanent' employees, by keeping this category as small as possible, owners were able to limit the financial consequences of the negotiated settlements.

These actions showed that despite obstacles and risks, workers could be stirred to open, collective protests. Internal divisiveness, lack of trust, and personal dependence remained, as did the personal dependence that influenced the course of events in *Action A*. The failed plan of several workers in a chemical enterprise to form a union and demand wage increases was another example.

The owner got a hint of the scheme through his chamchas (sycophants) who had long been in his employ. They had been brought by the owner when he moved from Mumbai to Bulsar and were given free lodging in the factory's compound and free firewood.[11] When the employer heard of the dissident workers' plans he immediately threatened to dismiss them. They abandoned their plan instantly.

The contribution made by several landowning workers to *Actions A* and *F* should be elaborated, however. The Dhodia who had been particularly active in *Action A* had enough land to receive sufficient income from farming to maintain his family. A trained Koli initiated *Action F*; another Koli, a technical school trainee, participated actively in the early phase of the strike. Although it would seem that Kolis would be the least prepared to participate in actions because of their economic and social position, the Gundlav stall keeper and organizer explicitly brought up the issue of the landowning workers' unwillingness to become involved in actions. While arguing that their broader subsistence base made them more easily satisfied with their wages, he seemed to forget that two landowning Kolis had worked with him in the GKM.

But one does not exclude the other: even given the active involvement of a landowning Dhodia in *Strike A* and two Kolis in *Strike F*. It is still possible that in general the landowning workers were more reticent to engage in such actions. If wages and working conditions were equally poor for all workers (*Actions A* and *F*), then the least vulnerable workers would be more likely to initiate action and could be stirred to open protest. They were more rapidly dissatisfied with low wages and poor working conditions, at the same time they were also more aware of their subordinate and vulnerable positions in such a firm.

In firms with differentials in wages and working conditions, those who occupied more favourable positions, particularly Kolis, would be less willing to participate in open protest. This applied all the more to cases where Dhodias, Dublas, Naikas, or Harijans (whom Kolis considered to be inferior) took the initiative.

ENTERPRISING ORGANIZERS

The organization of labour unions in the research area did not deviate from the pattern throughout India: small unions predominated. According to Myers and Kannappan (1970: 165) there were 6,594 registered labour unions in India, of which 70 per cent had fewer than 300 members in 1960. They attributed this trend to the law that allowed as few as seven persons to form a labour union and to have it officially registered. Between 1969 and 1974 in the small Bulsar taluka alone, four unions organized workers in the small-scale industry: the BDIEU, the SKS, and the GKM. An organizer from the taluka and the town of Dharampur located 30 km east of Bulsar led the fourth union. He began to recruit members from a rubber factory at Gundlav during 1974.

The second similarity between the local situation in Bulsar and the national one was the common background of labour leaders. In India labour unions are mainly led by outsiders. They come from urban middle class milieus and are allied with political parties. As a rule they operate independently of one another, each competing with other organizers in the same locale or firm (Myers and Kannappan, 1970: 175; Ramaswamy, 1973, 1974). In Bulsar none of the organizers originated from Bulsar taluka, but belonged to a higher socio-economic stratum than that of the workers and maintained contacts with local politicians. The secretary of the BDIEU had ties with the Congress-O party; the leader of the SKS supported the Jan Sangh; the leader of the GKM and the newcomer from Dharampur represented the Congress-R. The stall keeper activist who co-organized the Gundlav union had campaigned locally for the Congress-R candidate during the previous election.

Job actions initiated between the end of 1971 and early 1972 could be seen as related to the 1972 state Assembly elections. Initially the most prominent union leader was the secretary of the BDIEU (Congress-O). His actions may have been an attempt by the Congress-O to check the increasing popularity of Indira Gandhi (Congress-R) in south Gujarat, traditionally a bulwark of the then right-of-centre Congress-O party. The activities of the SKS leader conformed to the aims of the Jan Sangh, which was an advocate of the poorest of the poor. For instance, it organized a 'hunger march' as a protest against rising costs of living (Schenk-Sandbergen, 1975: 245). The party tried to win over the poorest people and their votes, fearing their growing radicalization.

The spontaneous job action in the Gundlav Engineering Factory erupted at the end of 1972, and the Gundlav union was founded in 1973. Although these events were not directly related to the elections, they did have a political dimension: the behavior of Congress-R activists in the strike supported Congress-R attempts to undermine Congress-O's hold in south Gujarat. The actions of the newcomer in Gundlav in 1974 had a similar goal: he said that he had been sent from the city of Surat to the small town of Dharampur to mobilize tribals, who constitute the bulk of the population in the eastern part of Bulsar district. He also organized a union in a rubber factory in Dharampur town, the only industrial enterprise in this sub-district.

For organizers the promotion of workers' interests was neither their primary concern nor only activity. They perceived unions to be a means of earning their livelihood, for managing a union did not differ from managing an enterprise. It required good relations with both employers and workers. Actually, union leaders fall into a range of different types. The leader of the BDIEU represented an extreme form of the self-aggrandizing type, while the SKS leader was less so. Even for him the workers in small industrial companies were only of secondary importance, as his primary focus was on Municipal workers and employees in other government establishments such as the railways.

Union leaders believed that small industrial firms in the region were unpromising venues for worker actions. Employees were too poorly paid to pay union dues. Further, because the small companies were financially very weak, union officials anticipated poor results for themselves and for the workers. Moreover, the wide dispersal of these companies made the time and energy required for regular attention not worthwhile. Most union leaders therefore preferred to concentrate on the more lucrative larger factories in the town of Bilimora and elsewhere in the district, or on government employees.

The formalized approach of union officials, which was based on regulations in the Factories Act, helped workers in factories. In these cases, only permanent workers were included in settlements. Since only permanent workers could join the unions, only a small portion of workers in small-scale industry saw their interests championed by organizers. Temporary workers employed in non-factories were the first victims of union-led action in their firms. If such workers participated in strikes or actions, they were dismissed. Therefore, union leaders tended to reinforce the differences between permanent and temporary workers.

The fact that the organizers were much like the brokers also undermined worker solidarity. Brokers were people who by virtue of their contacts with others controlled access to scarce resources. The political relations of organizers gave them links in government departments. These contacts enabled them to pressurize management and bind workers. At the same time, because of their grip on workers, they controlled labour for the management.

Such was the case with the SKS leader. After the settlement ending *Action E*, he was called upon by the management to iron out small conflicts. Furthermore, he brought 'troublesome' workers into line.

If a union leader was on good terms with employers it meant he had access to jobs. The SKS leader, for example, got workers employed elsewhere during *Action E*. As soon as the organizers established themselves in companies, they began to act as advocates for individual workers. Thus, the promotion of general worker interest increasingly assumed the character of favours distributed on an individual basis.

Good relations between union officials and management served workers well, provided workers did not cause problems.

WORKERS' IMPOTENCE

Actions indicated the small-industrial workers were discontent with wages and working conditions and they believed in collective action to improve them, but their consciousness did not extend beyond the individual firms. The actions were sporadic, and instigated by union leaders for opportunistic reasons. Industry-wide demonstrations against 'conditions in Bursar's small industrial companies' never occurred. Nor were there any sympathy actions in support of strikes in other companies. Even at Gundlav industrial estate such actions did not happen despite the concentration of enterprises and existence of a single union. Actually, Gundlav workers did not know what happened during *Action F*, nor what it was all about. Several factors account for this lack of general consciousness.

First, workers did not dare protest because an employer reacted harshly. If it was difficult to organize action to promote personal interests, it was even more difficult to mount action in support of others or on behalf of an abstract goal such as 'the improvement of the position of industrial workers'.

Second, relations between workers, employers, and others hindered development of a more general perspective. Recruitment and ensuing labour relations were personal, and discord or protest within any given firm was seen by others as an issue specific between those workers and their employer. Protesting workers themselves did not expect others to intervene in their conflict.

Third, the social and economic differences among workers had an effect. Differences in land ownership, lifestyle, social status and prestige could be overcome during an action. On the other hand, in everyday village life these factors determined identification, differentiation and behaviour.

The fourth factor was the procedures of union officials and their manipulation of dissatisfaction among workers. Personal political or economic gains were given priority by the organizers. Many leaders had little genuine sympathy for the workers they represented. Where they did have such sympathy, they directed their attacks towards individual firms. Moreover, because leaders wanted to force management to compromise, they could not build a general class-based front.

Workers considered the union leaders to be as corrupt as the government officials entrusted with the enforcement of labour legislation. Like civil servants, union leaders were alleged to be interested mostly in personal gain. Workers accused union leaders of making concessions after being paid by the management; organizers accused each other of the same. Furthermore, workers did not know whether union leadership indeed used the dues collected for the purpose it had been intended—like financing legal suits.[12] They charged the leaders of pocketing the money they collected to finance actions.

Other research information corroborated these findings: 'Unscrupulous union leadership in the past' (UNESCO, 1966: 183) caused workers in small-scale industries to be indifferent towards labour unions in Rajkot (Gujarat).

CONCLUSION

The final issue to be addressed is the position of small-scale industrial labour in the Indian production system. My information did not permit a reappraisal of the distinction between formal and informal sectors. There were differences among large industrial enterprises, government organizations, and industrial workshops and small factories, but they were quantitative, not qualitative. In the organized sector, too, an effective way to circumvent regulations was to keep many workers in temporary service (Breman, 1976: 113; Singh, 1973: 22, 23). Also, particularistic recruitment and personalized labour relations were not exclusive features of the small-scale sector. In large firms and government institutions as well, kinship, caste, friendship, and contacts with others were important in the recruitment of workers and in labour relations (Sheth, 1968; Bremen, 1979; Holmström, 1976; Hommes and Trivedi, 1979; van der Veen, 1979).

Wages of temporary workers in large concerns were similar to those of temporary workers in small companies. The prospect of a steady income for these workers was as poor as for those working in the small-scale sector.

Wage differentials did exist between permanent workers in large plants and permanent workers in small industrial companies. These differences could be found elsewhere in India, too. Holmström pointed out large differences in income and security between workers he studied in the four large and middle-sized concerns (Holström, 1976) and workers in small-scale industry.

During the same period of my fieldwork, Holmström (ibid.)

carried out research among south Indian factory workers in two large government enterprises, each with a few thousand workers, and two private firms, each with 500-600 employees.

> Unskilled, permanent workers in the latter concerns received a minimum of Rs. 269 per month (Rs. 10.34 per day). This included the basic wage, supplemented by a cost-of-living allowance, and a yearly bonus equal to 25 per cent of the basic wage plus cost-of-living allowance. (ibid., 59)
>
> Workers in Holmström's sample usually lived in solid two-room dwellings with electricity. Almost every home had a radio, a table, and a few chairs. Some had beds, a sewing machine, an electric fan, and a cooking-gas stove. Despite lack of privacy due to common washing and toilet facilities, the accommodation was good and the area healthy and calm. These neighbourhoods were certainly not slum-like. (ibid., 74)

Holmström classified these unskilled permanent workers as 'middle class'. Others, like Breman, described this category of workers as a labour elite. Workers employed under standard labour conditions and enjoying a relatively secure existence were a minority. They resembled salaried workers, according to Breman (1976: 36).

Still, I doubt whether these descriptions applied to all permanent workers in the organized sector. Tulpule (1971) argued against the idea that workers in the organized sector should be considered a privileged class. There were significant differences in working conditions and wages in different branches of industry.[13] Tulpule (ibid.) drew attention to poor housing, low status, absence of educational opportunities, and few opportunities for promotion. He also wrote that the pay was below the promised minimum wage. Moreover, these workers bore the burden of unemployed family members. Like Tulpule, Sau (1972) showed that between 1939 and 1969 the average real wages of factory workers earning less than Rs. 200 per month remained constant. This group includes 50 to 60 per cent of all Indian factory workers.

How should we define small-scale industrial labour? To begin with, small-scale industrial firms and their workers form an integral, if subordinate, part of Indian economic structure, and workers constitutes a heterogeneous category. The social and cultural differences attached to land ownership, as well as land ownership itself, were part of this heterogeneity. It prevented a single definition broad enough to cover all workers in the small-scale industry. Breman (1976:

39, 40, 43) distinguished the sub-proletariat as the largest segment in the urban labour system.

It included unskilled labourers who worked irregularly and for very low wages. They could not afford to stock provisions and ran their households in an ad-hoc manner. Their expenses were greater than their income; indebtedness was inevitable. This sub-proletariat was internally divided into smaller groups. The people felt impotent, insecure and stigmatized. Moreover, socially they made themselves dependent and lacked class-based organizations.

Indeed, these workers entirely depended on the sale of their labour power and can be characterized as sub-proletariat. However, this term does not include workers residing in villages (viz., rural non-agricultural labour), for the term is too 'urban'. Therefore, because this term is not appropriate for the rural part of the small-scale industrial labour—the *worker-peasants*—I reserve the term sub-proletariat for the urban workers.

The worker-peasants pointed, once again, to the inaccuracy of the idea of a 'dualistic' socio-economic system. Small-scale industrialization was based on peasants who used yields from their minor landholdings primarily for their personal consumption. It gave them the means to reproduce and enabled owners to keep wages low. The low wages attracted entrepreneurs who would invest in production; it also kept financially weak companies going. In turn, small-scale industry helped to keep the subsistence sector in agriculture going. Industrial earnings enabled members of worker-peasant households and families to hire irrigation pumps or buy better seeds, fertilizers, and pesticides. Thus, they were able to carry on their cultivation and remain in their villages.

NOTES

1. The maximum of Rs. 750,000 was the official criterion in the 1970s. Between 1971 and 2000 the maximum has been constantly raised.
2. Firms that are not subject to the regulations of the Factories Act are called non-factories.
3. A tea cup holds about 120 grams of uncooked rice.
4. See Breman, 1976: 27ff.
5. In Marxist literature, the emergence of a social class out of the same position

vis-à-vis the ownership of the means of production is described as the transition from a class in itself (*Class an sic*) to a class for itself (*Class Fr sic*). The awakening of the objective class position and its attendant organized promotion of interests are considered essential in this process.

6. Sanskritization is the familiar conceptualization to describe changes in lifestyle by members of lower castes, untouchables and tribals. See Srinivas (1962) and Mandelbaum (1970) for a more detailed treatment of Sanskritization.
7. In the late 1960s, the undivided Congress party split into two factions. Morarji Desai, who originated from a village near the town of Bulsar, headed the rightist faction, Congress-O. Indira Gandhi led the other faction, Congress-R.
8. Twice-born are from the three highest *varnas*, Brahmins, Kshatriyas and Banias, whose male members are allowed to wear the sacred thread. It refers to the sacred thread ceremony. This ceremony is the adolescent's initiation rite which is imagined as a second birth.
9. INTUC is an acronym for Indian National Trade Union Congress, which is affiliated to the Congress party.
10. Almost 46 per cent earned less than Rs. 4 per day and 21 per cent between Rs. 4 and 5 per day.
11. Like other Anavils the owners were timber merchants as well.
12. Workers usually paid the following amounts: Entrance fee of Re. 1 per person, monthly dues of Re. 1 per member, and levies to cover legal fees between Rs. 6-7 per person.
13. Singh (1973: 63) showed, for example, regional differences in wage levels in the textile industry.

CHAPTER 3

Reconsidering Bulsar Entrepreneurship

In the 1970s I concluded that:

> The results of the development of Bulsar's small industry are hardly encouraging . . . the development which grew primarily out of trade after 1960 is characterized by commercialism, the tendency to set up, successively or simultaneously, diverse commercial activities. . . . Commercialism has often been defined as an aspect of the transition to industrial capitalism from merchant capital. That can mean that commercialism is reducible to the business tradition of the new industrialists who are accustomed to easy profits on a short term. Undoubtly this orientation will not be without influence. But this is not a conclusive explanation because diversity in, and the spreading of, investment also occur among artisan entrepreneurs whose background might suggest otherwise. . . . Commercialism is thus not a characteristic of a special social group but inherent in the Indian socio-economic structure. In the first place, the extent of access to the government and community largely determines who is going to become involved in industrial production. Through these contacts investments in small-scale industry become possible and attractive, and they also allow entrepreneurs to profit from other lucrative possibilities. They can spread their risks, help close kin and others, and make timely reinvestments if profits decrease. . . . Despite their contacts, for many small-scale industrialists long-term entrepreneurship is uncertain. The overall economic structure encourages rather than prevents diverse investments and the spreading of risks. They—the owners of small industrial enterprises—cannot count on a regular supply of reasonably priced raw materials or on a constantly expanding market, after a short time a new and initially lucrative branch of industry is overcrowded. Betting on several horses is a rational entrepreneurial behaviour. (Streefkerk, 1985: 258, 259)

During the 1980s and the 1990s, authors challenged the applicability of the commercialism thesis and the distinction between merchant capitalists and productive capitalists.[1] I based the conclusion on the research I carried out among industrial entrepreneurs in Bulsar in 1971. They included Suthars, craftsmen; Anavil Brahmins, the traditional landowning caste of this area; and Vaishnava and Jain Banias, the merchants and businessmen. Commercialism was prevalent among them and it was most clearly manifested by the Jains. They owned the largest single number, 21 per cent, of the 143 small industrial enterprises in the research area. In the chapter on Jains, Plastics and Stationary (Streekerk, 1985: 156-62) I discussed their style of entrepreneurship, which is summarised below. In 1971, six Jains manufactured plastic items such as switches, containers, buckets, stationary, and small metal appliances in six separate firms. Five of the six firms use more or less identical hand presses employing electrically-heated moulds. They pressed plastic or metal raw material in order to produce the required shape. Technology and products of these firms were alike; close social relations between the owners of the six firms causing the similarity. They were from the same native area in Kutch, north-west Gujarat. Their grandfathers who were merchants and moneylenders lived in villages within 25 km of each other. Probably they belonged to the same *gol* (marriage circle). Their fathers migrated to Mumbai where they became grocers, owners of stationary stores, sold hardware, and invested in building construction. Their sons came to Bulsar where they opened industrial workshops.

Chain Electricals was the largest of these six firms. It was one of the larger units in the research area. The yearly turnover amounted to a few million rupees. There were about 60 workers. Electrical switches were the main product. The firm was owned by Shah, alias Switchwalla, and his family. They started manufacturing switches in Mumbai in the 1960s. The desire to broaden the family's economic base made them decide to go into industrial production. Contacts with a switch manufacturer gave Switchwalla the idea of entering the branch. It seemed 'easy and profitable'. At the same time they opened a stationary store and began, without success, the production of fountain pens. After all 'we are investors' as he put it. Or, 'we are not industrialists; we simply buy the machines and try to sell the plastic buckets,' as another owner of one of the six Jain firms confided.[2]

Because small-scale industrialization in Bulsar was still in its infancy in 1971, I found it difficult to predict exactly its future course, but I was not very optimistic. My idea was that, certainly in the initial stage when regular supply of raw material is uncertain and markets are imperfect, spreading of risks and commercialism indeed facilitate industrial investments. They require strategic contacts and sufficient capital, which are available only in a few selected groups. Access to these means of productions, however, also enables investors to redirect their pursuits of gains as soon as industrial profits decrease or when lucrative industrial enterprising is thwarted otherwise. The result would be industrialization without much continuity.

SWITCHWALLA IN 1990

I explored my earlier characterization of entrepreneurship and assessment of small-scale industrial development in 1990. General tendencies, described in the earlier chapter, aroused my doubts. These tendencies included: The enormous expansion of the town's population from 55,000 inhabitants in 1971 to an estimated number of more than 1,00,000 inhabitants in 1990. Second, the emergence of a middle class and the changed power structure of the town. And finally, the considerable rise in the number of industrial establishments. They were located mostly at the huge GIDC industrial estate at Vapi, 30 km to the south of Bulsar towards the Maharashtra-Gujarat border.[3] In the immediate vicinity of Bulsar, along the NH 8 and the two state highways, many small-scale and medium sized industries, owned or managed by people from Mumbai too, had come into existence during the last decade as well. The number of establishments at the Gundlav GIDC industrial estate along one of these roads, 3 km to the east of Bulsar, had also increased. After 1985 the estate had been extended on the other side of the road. In 1990 the old and new part together accommodated 183 firms; in 1971 there were only 16 enterprises. Many of the 143 firms which in the beginning of the 1970s were spread over the town and its vicinity had disappeared. Suthars closed their bobbin factories and many units owned by Anavils, Banias and others had also vanished. Of the 16 establishments which were started at the nearby Gundlav industrial estate in the same period, only 4 were still present in 1990; 9 had disappeared and 3 had been bogus firms.

The closure of factories by itself is not a sufficient proof of the validity of the idea that commercialism leads to unstable industrial development. Whether or not these enterprises were part of a series of successive or simultaneous business activities and why they had been closed is decisive information.

To collect this information the research concentrated on the Gundlav industrial estate; the tracing of closed factories and their owners outside the estate would have taken too much time. One of the 'survivors' at Gundlav helped with the reconstruction. His general information and my knowledge about industries and their owners at the beginning of the 1970s at Gundlav hardly differed. At least seven of the nine industrial firms which had closed down were not part of other industrial or commercial activities. The industrial firms at Gundlav were the owners' only source of income. They failed due to a combination of technological, financial, commercial and personal reasons. One died without offspring, the second was murdered; others disappeared; one of them migrated to Canada. The eighth enterprise, part of a larger concern, was first sold and then closed because the new owners were not really interested and managed the firm badly. The ninth factory was a daughter concern of an enterprise in Mumbai. Labour troubles made the owners decide to wind-up the factory. Of the four enterprises that still existed in 1990, two were part of commercial and industrial undertakings based in Mumbai. The majority of the factories established in the early 1970s at Gundlav collapsed because the owners failed as entrepreneurs. My informant who, like others faced serious difficulties in the beginning, phrased these failures as follows: 'Here—at Gundlav and in India—many starting industrialists have fancy ideas, but they lack practicality... Some made the mistake to develop their own machines, which took time and money without sufficient income. While a few years later they could have imported or bought these machines.'

The most important reason to doubt the original assessment of the type of entrepreneurship and quality of industrialization was the history of Switchwalla and his family, owners of Chain Electricals. The family concern expanded between 1971 and 1990 to become the largest producer of plastic switches and allied products. The assortment of products included different items such as numerous types of switches, 'light dimmers, fan regulators, circuit breakers, fuse links as well as musical door bells'. A few years earlier electric irons, bulbs and tubes were added. Furthermore, one of the sons began to manufacture cosmetics. The concern consisted of numerous small factories dispersed all over south Gujarat. Some of these were established in towns such as Bulsar, Bilimora, and Navsari while others were located in the countryside. Tubes and bulbs were manufactured in establishments situated in Chennai and Hydrabad. The family became major shareholders of these factories in 1985 and since then products have been sold under the brand name of Chain.

I am not sure about the precise number of undertakings, Switchwalla cited 20 while his sons said they owned 40 enterprises. These differences in number can apparently be explained by differences in ownership. Many of these enterprises were 'officially' owned not by the family but by the managers of the units, so as to avoid tax and labour laws. According to Switchwalla, numerous small firms were easier to manage then a few large ones. He claimed that his success was due to the quality of his products, good advertising and competitive prices.

The production process in most of the units was, like in the 1970s, based primarily on hand presses and manual labour. It was labour intensive, not so complicated, and thus cheap. According to the management, the concern employed a total of 5,000 workers, but the actual number was probably much more. Most of the workers were women belonging to all age groups. The explanation offered in the head office in Mumbai and by some managers in Bulsar was that women were pre-eminently suited for the delicate work by hand required for the job. Furthermore, women were cheaper than men and the labour turnover among them was less because 'the Indian woman is strongly tied to the house'. Moreover, girls and women from the villages liked to work in the factories because they could contribute to the incomes of their households without having to work in the field, which was much heavier, offered less freedom and paid less.

I visited a few Chain firms in Bulsar. One employed 8 men and 100 women who all assembled switch parts. Another was an engineering workshop which employed not more than 9 persons, so that it would not come under the purview of the Factories Act. It produced copper parts of switches with the help of powered presses. According to the supervisor of the large enterprise, some of the workers were employed permanently and others as 'helpers'. Permanent workers had the rights to bonus, paid leave and provident fund. Their wage was Rs. 17 or 18 per day (in 1990 the official minimum wage was Rs. 21). They sometimes earned more (Rs. 20 to 25) because their wage was supplemented by piece rate. 'Helpers' were temporary workers, they earned less and were not eligible for the just mentioned facilities. The factories ran six days a week for nine hours a day. Unlike other factories at Gundlav, there were no night-shifts so that women did not have to travel after dark. Since I did not have the opportunity to compare this information with what the women themselves said about the conditions of their work, the information must be handled with caution. In any case, the factories looked neat and tidy. Further, the women had their own toilet facilities. Taps enabled them to wash themselves and keep their tiffin boxes clean. They came from neighbouring villages and were mostly Kolis and tribals like Dhodias or Dublas.[4] (Field notes)

One of the most remarkable sections of the chain concern was the great distribution centre just outside Bulsar. The centre was located at the spot where Switchwalla and his brother had begun their factory in 1968. Around 1980 they shifted the workshop to the Gundlav industrial estate and built a few sturdy warehouses at the site. All finished, semi-processed products, and raw materials from various parts of India were collected and stored there. The goods were subsequently sent to clients or to factories which worked on the raw materials or semi-processed products. The transport of these goods was organized by the management itself. More than 20 trucks drove the goods from suppliers to Bulsar, and from Bulsar to factories and clients all over India. The centre employed 200 employees. The history of the Switchwalla family and the information about first generation entrepreneurs at Gundlav are too selective to draw conclusions. However, the case of Switchwalla together with the general development of Bulsar and its vicinity certainly do provide grounds to rethink the opinion of small-scale industrial development.

The closed enterprises at Gundlav showed that the first stage of industrial entrepreneurship was a difficult period and that it was problematic to use information about this period as evidence for the style of entrepreneurship. The history of the Switchwallas revealed that commercialism did not necessarily lead to an unstable industrial development. Switchwalla's entrepreneurship did not differ from my earlier description. Also, in 1990 he, and other owners, claimed that 'horizontal diversification', or what I termed 'betting on different horses', was an important condition for successful entrepreneurship. Open for debate, therefore, was my assessment[5] of industrial development which I had based on this type of entrepreneurship. The discussion could stress the greater weight of ideas in evaluating a phenomenon than in describing it. But in terms of detachment the difference between evaluation and description is not so clearly marked. Neither describing a phenomenon, nor appraising it, happens independently of the views of the researcher.

The researcher as research instrument, is a characteristic of anthropological fieldwork. The different stages of the research procedure are combined within one person. That's why the gathering of data, their analysis and evaluation are highly sensitive to the personality, perception, and theories of the fieldworker. Moreover, the study of small-scale industries lends itself pre-eminently to projections of the ideas of the fieldworker. Sandesara (1988: 644) points out that the small-scale industrial development is susceptible to several interpretations: 'one can say almost anything, even statistically, ranging from the most complimentary to the most derogatory, on small industry'.

CONCLUSION

The history of Switchwalla and his family, and recent developments in Bulsar did not fit in my original discourse on entrepreneurship and industrial development. My initial theoretical preferences and methodology, together with the ideological climate in Amsterdam, and the prevailing discussions over development and underdevelopment, excluded processes which had occurred in south Gujarat during the 1970s and 1980s. More specifically, my earlier anti-capitalist perspective offered little room for a more sympathetic appraisal of entrepreneurs and their achievements. It is manifested in taken-for-granted coupling of the style of entrepreneurship and the supposed inferior quality of industrialization. The first can still stand empirical test, the latter requires reconsideration. The conclusion that this style of entrepreneurship necessarily leads to uncertain and unstable industrial development needs re-examination.

The question that remained to be answered was whether this reappraisal was based on the 1990 situation alone or on other considerations as well. The 'Bulsar of 1990' had indeed amazed me, but it had not taken me totally by surprise. The expansion of the town, the industrial situation, and the history of Switchwallas provided food for doubts which I had harboured already for some time. They arose from a combination of personal experiences and other academic insights. These made me, among other things, more aloof and led me to reconsider my ideas.

Research in the 1970s clarified that modernization theories on entrepreneurship *en-vogue* then could not be applied in south Gujarat (Streefkerk, 1985). Owners of small industrial enterprises in the area did not belong to minorities or culturally marginal groups who, therefore, had been able to break through 'traditional ways of doing things'. Neither did they originate from groups experiencing changing social status which, due to ensuing social and cultural ambiguities, could create innovative personalities.

Those who dominate industrial transition in south Gujarat since the early 1970s belong to groups who have been in the centre of south Gujarat's urban and rural economic, political, social and cultural life since long. It is precisely their predominance which provides access to finance, administration, skills, raw material, labour, and customers, required to set up and run industrial enterprises. Artisans, who are of a more modest social origin, are also well integrated in south Gujarat's towns and villages. They could participate because of their technical skills.

For all groups participating in the industrial transition it is clear that entrepreneurship is a collective phenomenon which cannot be understood in terms of individual motivations and actions. Caste and kinship provide business people the social capital required for successful entrepreneurship. Primordial ties offer access to, and control over skills, administration, markets, capital and labour. The ideas and structure of caste are, instead of being eroded, crucial in the mobilization and monopolization of resources, and the recruitment and control of labour.

From the 1970s onwards the quality of industrial entrepreneurship became the major academic issue. Its supply, i.e. its volume, was no longer considered to be a major bottleneck. The second main strand in the debate on the question of industrial entrepreneurship, the structural perspective, made itself felt.

This changed perspective leaned heavily on the emerging Marxist-inspired critique of the modernization approach. The critique maintained that worldwide capitalist expansion during the last two to three centuries brought underdevelopment to Africa, Latin-America and Asia. In the international academic milieu *the development of underdevelopment* became common knowledge. In other words, India's political-economy had to be explained in terms of structural dependency and subordination which hampered long-term industrial capital formation and gave way to handicapped or 'deformed' industrial entrepreneurs.

I called the deformed nature of industrial entrepreneurship 'commercialism' and used the concept to analyse industrial transition in south Gujarat. The term refers to the inclination of entrepreneurs to invest successively and simultaneously into wide range of disparate commercial and industrial ventures. This attitude implies extreme exploitation of labour and redirecting of investments as soon as industrial profits decrease. Betting on several horses is a rational entrepreneurial behaviour, but it results in industrialization without much continuity. This attitude had often been perceived as part of the transition from merchant capital to industrial capitalism which, indeed, has been the dominant transfer in Gujarat. Commercialism was, thus, reduced to the business tradition of the new industrial entrepreneurs who had been used to 'easy profits on a short term'. However, the commercial style of industrial entrepreneurship could not be sufficiently explained by the tradition of a specific group. Among successful artisan entrepreneurs, whose background might suggest otherwise, the same tendency could be observed. Though generally artisans lacked finance and social contacts to widen the scope of their investments, commercialism had to be seen as the consequence of the over-all socio-economic structure which, because of the insecure supply of raw materials and the lack constantly expanding markets, encouraged rather than prevented diverse investments and spreading of risks (Streefkerk, 1985). During the 1980s and 1990s authors challenged the applicability of the commercialism thesis and the distinction between merchant capitalists and productive capitalists.[6]

Despite ideological differences and related distinct theoretical perspectives the cultural and structural approaches are similar in their questioning of the possibility of long-term employment of capital and labour for industrial purposes in countries like India. The over-all similarity can be explained by the common background of the originators of these ideas. Marx and Weber were inspired by what happened in Europe during their lifetimes in which capitalist modernity was seen as the prerogative of the West (Sayer, 1991:

14, 109). However, to blame these two founder-fathers of Western sociology and anthropology would be too an easy excuse for skepticism about long-term industrial enterprise in countries like India. In a recent treatise on entrepreneurship in Asia and the West, Rutten (1994b: 46) argues against the danger of 'mirroring' Asian capitalists against their European counterparts. The perceived 'pseudo- or non-genuine capitalist nature of the present South and South-East Asian entrepreneurs is partly based on postulates about the origins and nature of European industrialists of which the validity is seldomly questioned.[7] By challenging the theoretical and empirical validity of the assumptions of European capitalists he points to the distorted view on these entrepreneurs and simultaneously shows the ethnocentric perspective on Asian entrepreneurship.

NOTES

1. Harris, 1982; Holström, 1984; Rutten, 1991 and 1994; and Gorter 1994.
2. The narration of Papu, the Jain stock-broker from Mumbai in Naipaul's *India, A Million Mutinies Now* (1990: 11) shows that, despite much evidence to the contrary, the idea that Jains are not suitable for industrial entrepreneurship is still alive. He says, 'We are traders. . . . The killer instinct is required in industry, not in trading. Which is why the Jain community is not involved in industry. If I'm trading in the stock exchange now, and I cannot get some money from the guy, I wouldn't hire a mafia guy to get it out of him. Which is what happens here in something like the building-industry. . . .'
3. Several industrial townships came up between 1970 and 1990 in the southern-most part of south Gujarat; Vapi is the largest.
4. In chapters 5 and 6, I present a different picture of the labour conditions in Chain Elecricals.
5. I do not use the term analysis because of its suggestion of objectivity.
6. Harriss, 1982; Holmström, 1984; Rutten, 1991 and 1994; Gorter, 1994.
7. In their recent publication on the economic history of the Netherlands between 1500–1815, De Vries and Van der Woude (1995: 205-213) argue that the Weberian connection between Calvinism and capitalist-rational ethics is difficult to prove for the Netherlands in this period.

CHAPTER 4

Capitalist Modernity and Caste: The Suthars

Curiosity to know about how Suthars had fared during the 1970s and 1980s brought me to Bulsar in 1990. Suthars were part of my research in 1970 and 1974 because they played a major role in the early industrial development of Bulsar and of other small south Gujarati towns. They were among the first to start industrial workshops and small factories (Streefkerk, 1985: 68-128).

SUTHARS: THE GENESIS OF AN URBAN CASTE

In south Gujarat and Bulsar, Suthars and Luhars formed one single endogamous category or, in the words of A.M. Shah, a caste division of the first order (Shah, 1982: 5). In 1971 there were at least 250 Suthar households and probably 25 Luhar households (Streefkerk, 1985: 98). Names of several areas in the old part of the town, like Suthar Chawl and Luhar Tekra, suggested a second-order division between Suthars and Luhars. However, this distinction was anything but clear. Some Suthars considered themselves to be superior to Luhars. They believed that working on iron was more crude and polluting than carpentry work; that Luhars ate non-vegetarian food; that they had the habit of drinking liquor. Furthermore, they maintained that Luhar women could marry Suthar men, but they did not appreciate the reverse. For the youngest generation these ideas belonged to the past. In 1990 there were 425 Suthar households. The number was given by the leaders of the Shree Panchal Seva Samaj. They did not distinguish between Suthars and Luhars.

The interchangeability of both occupations in villages and towns, a trait already noted by Gadgil in 1924 (1973: 173), contributed to the disappearance of the distinction between Suthars and Luhars. Moreover, the work of Carpenters and Blacksmiths frequently complemented one another, as for example, in the manufacture of agricultural tools and means of transport. At least a few Suthars were aware that their grandfathers had switched over from working on iron to wood or combined both when making bullock carts. Emerging occupational diversity among Suthars and Luhars further eroded the distinction among them. This chapter details the dominant habit in Bulsar and treats Suthars and Luhars together, and calls them Suthars.

In 1990 the Suthars were an 'urban caste'. Several of them resided in villages adjoining Bulsar Municipality which belonged to the urban agglomeration of Bulsar. Suthars claimed to have no ties with their natal villages, and have long since stopped visiting them. They no longer had family property there, and their original *kaccha* houses had disappeared. Around 1900 there was a massive migration of Suthars, and others, from their villages in south Gujarat. It is said that this exodus was caused by an influenza epidemic and a famine during these years; a fact confirmed by Mukhtyar (1930: 51) for the village of Atgam. Already, before 1900 Suthars and other artisans left their villages because of growing poverty due to the inadequacy of their wages which were paid partly in kind[1] (Streefkerk, 1985: 75). They migrated to other villages or towns. After 1900 Suthars also went to East Africa and the Fiji's (Streefkerk: 114). The third type of migration was from villages to smaller towns like Bulsar or Navsari, and from towns to the cities of Ahmedabad, Baroda, and Mumbai. They stayed there temporary and returned to their native region again. The return did not mean the severance of ties with these cities. Almost all Suthar families in Bulsar had near or distant relatives who lived and worked in Mumbai, Ahmedabad, or Vadodara.

In Bulsar and Mumbai Suthars earned a living as building contractors; furniture makers, general carpenters, metal workers in small repair workshops. In Bulsar, the railways employed them as carpenters, blacksmiths, fitters and turners.

Before Independence, the Railway Company was one of the major employers in Bulsar; Anavils took hold of the white-collar jobs. Suthars and Luhars worked as carpenters or performed engineering jobs in the maintenance of the wooden coaches and engines, and some became engine drivers. Employment in the Railway Company meant being transferred from Bulsar to other stations along the railway line. The Railway Company thus was a cause of migration among the Suthars. It offered economic security and favourable secondary benefits.

Building contracting and furniture making were the most lucrative occupations. Suthars were the major contractors between 1930 and 1970 in the town. They built houses of well-to-do inhabitants, like Banias, Parsis and Desais. They also built the wooden bungalows of the Railway Colony. They accomodated European employees of the British-controlled Railway Company. After Independence, in 1955, one of them built the townhall of Bulsar. Later on, in the late 1960s, they constructed the modern bungalows of the newly-developed cooperative housing societies outside the old centre of town, its the first major extension after 1947.

Since 1930 Suthars owned several furniture workshops in Bulsar. One family combined building contracting and the making of furniture. Several Suthars and Luhars started small engineering workshops in the 1930s and 1940s but their opportunities were restricted. Neither the town's economy nor the agriculture in the surrounding villages offered much scope for this kind of metal work (Streefkerk, 1985: 78, 79). Suthars improved their economic situation of between 1910 and the Second World War in Bulsar. An elite emerged which built its houses outside the town in the 1930s, they are still witnesses to their prosperity. Many other Suthars later settled in these areas. Some others resided in the old part of the town, where they still own houses and land.

Suthar families who were well-to-do were a small minority. Many became carpenters or workers in the firms and workshops owned by their caste fellows. Others had to be content with simple jobs in the railways, which earned them modest incomes. Many could not afford to buy land and build their own houses.

In the 1940s some Suthars started bobbin factories. They were the pioneers of industrial production in Bulsar.

They owned about eight bobbin firms between 1941 and 1965. During the Second World War, the demand for wooden bobbins used in the textile industry in Mumbai, Surat and Ahmedebad increased. Imports from England and Japan were cut off. At the same time the production of textiles grew considerably due to the demand from the Indian Army.

The local demand also increased because imported textiles were no longer available. Between 1950 and 1960 production of wooden bobbins in Bulsar expanded further. Following the Second World War, the Indian textile industry expanded with an increase in the range of textile manufactured, partly due to the introduction of synthetic fibers.

The availability of wood facilitated the production of wooden bobbins in Bulsar. Traditionally the town had been a centre for timber trade; the nearby forests guaranteed a regular supply of wood.

Suthars' familiarity with wood working and the comparative low expenses to start bobbin production added to the transition. Capital was supplied by Banias and Suthars themselves; labour was provided by family members and poor caste-fellows.[2] Thus, the production of bobbins became a main feature of the town's economy in the 1950s and 1960s. Its significance is marked by a Suthar's chairmanship of Bulsar's Municipal Council in the early 1950s. It was during this period that a Suthar contractor built the townhall.

The establishment in the 1950s of the Atul Chemical Complex, 7 km to the south of Bulsar, and the fact that the town became district headquarters in 1964, created new opportunities for Suthars. It meant a greater occupational range for them. More Suthars became part of the town's incipient middle class. At that time, the youngest generation was better educated compared to their fathers and uncles. Through the presence of family members in Mumbai and other cities, they were able follow higher education and special courses outside Bulsar. Some of them became graduates in chemical and civil engineering, or completed other engineering courses. Several of them got responsible jobs in Atul, or were absorbed as engineers in the higher ranks of the expanding state administration in Bulsar and elsewhere in Gujarat. But still, for many the railways were an important employer.

Several Suthars profited from the new opportunities as private entrepreneurs. Suthar contractors were engaged in the construction and maintenance of the Atul Complex, which included residential quarters. One of them got the contract to fabricate the wooden furniture and equipment used in the Atul Complex. Another opened the town's first general store, selling provisions to the higher personnel of Atul. The latter generally had a more cosmopolitan background than the inhabitants of Bulsar. Migration remained a salient feature. Suthars went to Mumbai and other cities, where they were employed by private industrial concerns, started their own workshops, or became contractors. One of them went from Bulsar to Kolkata, where he became a successful architect.

THE DISAPPEARANCE OF SUTHAR FIRMS BETWEEN 1970 AND 1990

In 1971 and 1974, I studied Suthars from the perspective of Bulsar's industrial development. They were an example of local craftsmen and petty producers who accomplished the transition to industrial production through the manufacture of bobbins. I compared this process, which stagnated from the late 1960s onwards, with the developments among Suthars and other artisans in the neighbouring town of Bilimora. There, the transition was far more spectacular: Its artisans manufactured deep-well pumps and other agricultural implements, textile machinery, and other engineering products. The political-historical differences between the two towns explains the divergent industrial development of Suthars in Bulsar and their caste-fellows and members of other artisan castes in Bilimora. The other explanation was close linkage between industrial development in Bilimora and the more fertile and prosperous agricultural environment of the town (Streefkerk, 1985: 105-25). Recent developments among Suthars in Bulsar, discussed in the second part of this chapter, confirm the relation between more well-to-do farmers and industrialization among local artisans. First, the chapter discusses the fate of the bobbin industries in the 1980s and 1990s.

The quick increase in the number of producers of wooden bobbins in Bulsar between 1940 and 1971 caused profits to decline. Most of the 12 bobbin firms in 1970, were 'subsistence firms'; they did not grow and prosper, but subsisted (Streefkerk: 87-90). The precarious position of bobbin industries in the early 1970s was still further weakened by the rising prices of wood and the decreased demand for the traditional wooden bobbins. The first was the result of the official policy to protect the forests. The second was caused by the use of synthetic bobbins by the textile industry. In the early 1980s, the Suthar owners closed their factories. Among these factories were two firms which were the largest in 1971.

Mistry Wood Works stopped production after its 85-years old

founder expired in 1982. The founder had two sons, one lived in Mumbai and the other in Bulsar. The son in Mumbai is on bad terms with his family in Bulsar.

The son in Bulsar, about 48-years old, did not want to continue the production. He closed the factory and lived off his share of the ancestral property in Bulsar, including several houses given on rent. He had four daughters and a son. Two daughters were married to Suthars. One of them lived in Ahmedabad and the other migrated to the USA. The third daughter will migrate to Portugal to marry a Mochi from Bulsar. The latter's family migrated to Mozambique when the country belonged to Portugal. The fourth daughter and the only son, the youngest, attended secondary school.

Vishwakarma Engineering, the oldest bobbin factory in Bulsar, was closed also in the early 1980s. Between 1950 and 1970 it was one of the most prosperous firms, but in the 1970s the manufacture of bobbins was not really profitable any longer, and the owner grew old. He closed the factory which was situated in one of the main streets of the town. By selling the land he added many lakhs of rupees to his wealth. He had four sons, two of them stayed in the USA, one was an engineer in a textile company in Mumbai and the fourth son owned a lodge in Bulsar.

In 1990 there were seven bobbin workshops in Bulsar. Suthars possessed two of them, two other artisans owned the other two, and the fifth was owned by a Brahmin. Already in 1971 they were small firms, between 1971 and 1990 they did not grow. In 1990 they employed seven or eight workers on a daily basis. Thus, the workers were kept outside the purview of labour legislation. Yet, these 'temporary hands' served the same Suthars for two decades. Twenty years later they recognized when I visited the workshops.

The two Suthar firms were the only workshops left from the six Suthar factories in operation in 1971. Bobbins were one of the products manufactured in one of them. Wooden handles of screwdrivers and chisels were the other products.

Well-to-do Suthars described the owners and their families as 'not rich, not poor'. They did not have cars, nor telephone connections. But they owned houses and had landed property in Bulsar. One of them had built a three-storied house on his property.

Dhodias owned the remaining two bobbin workshops. They were former employees of a bobbin factory which was closed several years earlier by its Bania owner. They took over the inventory and started doing job-work for other bobbin manufacturers in Bulsar.

Suthar industrial pioneers vanished from the industrial scene in Bulsar between 1980 and 1990. Their disappearance is best exemplified by the end of the engineering company Quality Transformers Pvt Ltd.

In the late 1960s it was one of the larger engineering enterprises in Bulsar, manufacturing transformers. Four cousins of a prominent bobbin factory owned the enterprise (Streefkerk: 95-6). From its start in 1961, the factory ran far below its capacity. The Suthars faced difficulties in procuring raw material; they needed an import license, and were unable to book sufficient orders.

In 1973 the majority of the factory's shares was taken over by a family member from the neighbouring town of Bilimora. He was one of the successful Suthars there, owning several large metal-working enterprises. The Bulsar unit was to do job-work for the Bilimora enterprises. A few years later the company was liquidated.

Two of the four original partners expired, the third served in a Suthar company in Bilimora. The fourth was sales manager in a paper-manufacturing company located in Bilimora too.

The son of one of the expired partners ran a small scooter and motorbike repair shop in Bulsar. His brother worked in an enginering company in Mumbai.

The sons of the other expired partner served in industrial companies in Mumbai. One of them commuted daily between Mumbai and Bulsar. He was proprietor of a tiny workshop, Electrical Sound Industries, in Bulsar. A skilled worker operated the only lathe. He repaired and made sound equipment, and transformers.

The sons of the owners of the remaining wood-working enterprises did not rejuvenate Suthar industrial entrepreneurship in Bulsar. They were salaried employees, serving as chemists, draughtsmen or engineers in industrial enterprises at Vapi. Others were partners in their father's firms. They helped to keep the firms going and earned a reasonable income. But the firms remained subsistence enterprises, which did not prosper or grow.

A GENERATION OF NEW ENTREPRENEURS

In the village Segvi were some young Suthar entrepreneurs. The village belonged to the urban agglomeration of Bulsar. It was located along the road leading to the Tithal beach, a few kilometres to the west of Bulsar. It accommodated several families of artisans who owned industrial workshops. Among them were a few Kumbhar families, one family ran a saw-mill. Suthars owned most of the workshops. One family ran two engineering firms. The owners were able to fabricate many products like chemical equipment, steel furniture, metal sheets, pipes, frames, and dies for brick manufacturers. Despite this impressive range of products, the performance of the family enterprise was poor in 1990.

The firms of other Suthars were certainly more well-to-do. One of them manufactured wooden furniture and wooden equipment used by Atul and its sister concerns. The owners of two other firms both sold tractors of two different brands. They also manufactured trailers and agricultural equipment. These two large families, Jeepwalas and Panchals, as I will call them, were neighbours. The Jeepwalas stayed in three separate households in three different houses. The Panchals lived in one house and shared one kitchen. The two families descended from one great-grand father who was a carpenter in Segvi. Their two grandfathers were also carpenters, who used to make wooden frames of the houses in Segvi and nearby villages.

The Jeepwala family included two generations in 1990. The eldest generation consisted of four brothers, sons of the fore-mentioned grandfather. They stayed in Segvi, earning a living by making and repairing horse carts and bullock carts. Their ages were between 74 and 53. Three brothers migrated to Mumbai. One of them was an engineer in the Mumbai Municipal Corporation, the other a designer and the third was an architect.

The youngest generation consisted of the sons and children of the four brothers who remained in Segvi, and a son of one of the Mumbai-brothers. The age of these cousins varied between 25 and 40 years.

The Panchals were made up of three generations. The eldest in the family was the grandfather, a cousin of the expired grandfather of the Jeepwalas. His bullock carts and horse carts were known all over south Gujarat. His four brothers migrated to other towns and villages in south Gujarat.

The second generation included the eight sons of the grandfather. Three of them lived in Segvi; they were between 35 and 55 years of age. Four sons migrated to Mumbai where they were all employed in technical occupations. The eighth brother owned a small engineering workshop in Bilimora.

The children of the brothers living in Segvi constitute the third generation. Their age varies between 14 and 35 years.

The early 1970s were crucial years for the two families. Till then they manufactured and repaired traditional agricultural implements and means of conveyance, like bullock carts, horse carts and hand carts. Between 1972 and 1974, they changed over to the production of tractor trailers, iron ploughs, levelers of land and other heavy agricultural equipment. The production of trailers and implements meant a definite change in the techniques of production. Work on metal, like pressing, fitting, turning and welding came to predominate. Some machines, like a large metal-press, were made by themselves.

In each family labour was divided between brothers and cousins. Some were responsible for the production of trailers and equipment, others were in charge of sales. So, in the beginning, the youngest of the four brothers of the Jeepwala family travelled on motorbike throughout south Gujarat, including the prosperous Bardoli taluka, to visit the villages and convince farmers to buy their products.

In the early 1980s the third generation of Jeepwalas and Panchals entered the family enterprises. The two families began to sell tractors. Jeepwalas had been more successful salesmen than the Panchals. The former became the sole selling agents of a prominent brand of tractors in Bulsar district. They were approached by a representative of this brand because of their access to the farmers of south Gujarat. Jeepwallas and Panchals 'officially' employed 9 to 10 workers in their workshops. They were Kolis, Dhodias and Dublas from Segvi trained on the spot. Some of the Dubla workers were from families who, according to the Suthars, 'belonged' to their families for several generations. They resided in the compounds of the Jeepwalas and Panchals.

'Initially we sold equipments, then tractors; now we sell tractors plus equipment,' said the Jeepwala who managed the tractor agency.

He was a science graduate, educated in Mumbai and driving force behind the enterprise. The head office of the agency was in Bulsar. They ran a service station near Gundlav, opened in 1987. In 1988 they started a branch office in Navsari. A cousin brother, son of an uncle in Mumbai, ran the agency in Navsari.

The sales of tractors steadily increased between 1981 and 1990. In 1982 they sold 94 tractors; in 1989-90 the number was 125.

The manager stressed that in order to accommodate family members and to spread financial risks, diversification of interests is a must. Thus the family also traded in building material.

The family enterprise of the Panchals expanded too. In 1982 they acquired a tractor-agency in Bulsar. It had a early turnover of about 25 tractors. In Bilimora they started a workshop for production of trailers, ploughs and other agricultural instruments.

The examples of the Jeepwalas and Panchals again showed the close relation between agricultural developments and the rise of local entrepreneurship from the ranks of artisans (Saberwal, 1976: 19, 136, 137; Streefkerk, 1985: 124, 257). Canal irrigation in south Gujarat expanded when the Jeepwalas and Panchals started producing heavy agricultural implements and began selling tractors. In 1990 canal irrigation covered almost the whole of the district. With the increase of canal irrigation the mechanization, or tractorization of agriculture advanced and heavier agricultural equipment could be used.[3] The government assisted farmers financially to buy tractors to stimulate tractorization. Farmers who owned at least 8 acres of irrigated land were eligible for government support. In short, in a mainly agrarian environment, longterm entrepreneurial successes of urban Suthars and other artisans depend on developments in the villages.

SUTHAR RANK

To position Suthars within the urban class structure I used the town's telephone directory. The method was quick, cheap and rewarding. In 1900, a telephone connection was a luxury, names in the directory indicated prosperity. The directory could be used to describe the contours of the economic elite within a certain area; to trace the material differences between members of different castes; and to outline the economic elite within castes, provided that surnames are the monopoly of a specific caste. The names of Mistry, Panchal and Sanghadia, used by Suthars in Bulsar, fulfilled this condition.

Formerly, certainly in villages, people did not use surnames. In 1990 surnames were instrumental in claims for higher status. Kumbhars (potters), for instance, call themselves Prajapati, Khatri (cotton weavers) are known as Kapadia (cloth merchant), and Bhangi (sweeper) often use the surname Solanki. Some names are so widely used by members of different first-order social divisions, that they do not indicate, or rather hide the social background of its bearer. The surname Patel is an example; the name is used by Patidar, Kanbi, Koli and tribal categories such Dhodia.

Suthars in Bulsar called themselves Mistry, which means carpenter or contractor. Sometimes the name was used by others who were in construction business. In Bulsar, Suthars also called themselves Panchal, but they were a minority. Elsewhere, for instance in Bilimora and in central Gujarat, the name Panchal was found more frequently. Only a few Suthar families in Bulsar used the name Sanghadia. I checked the list of names and telephone numbers together with some well-informed Suthars. It appeared that only six Mistry were not Suthars. They were contractors, some of them were Muslims, one was a Koli.

According to the 1988 Telephone Directory (Bulsar Telecommunication District: 200, 201, 203, 208), there were 44 telephone connections among the 425 Suthar households in Bulsar and the adjoining villages; a density of 10.8 per cent. The 44 connections consisted of residential phones and phones in private offices. The number of connections in another artisan caste, the Kumbhars, called Prajapati and Lad, was 24. The density among them was probably lower than among Suthars, because there were more than 250 Kumbhar households in Bulsar.

The telephone density among Suthars also had to be compared with the proportion of telephones among groups who made up the economic establishment of the town. For this purpose I used the number of telephone connections of Anavils. They used the surnames Desai, Naik and Vashi. In south Gujarat, the name Desai was the monopoly of Anavils and was most common among them. The name was also used in other parts of western India, like Maharashtra. If there were such Desais in Bulsar, there were few of them. Anavils also used the names Naik and Vashi.

There were 201 connections among 1,500 Anavil households in Bulsar and the adjoining villages (ibid.: 184-7, 202, 217). It was a density of 13.4 per cent.

The figures had to be treated carefully. Because its capacity was limited, the Bulsar District Telephone Exchange had not been able to meet the many demands for connections since many years. To present a more valid picture, the number of applications of Anavils and Suthars should have been taken into account too, but these data were not available. Anyhow, the little difference between the proportion of telephone connections of Anavils and Suthars might indicate the socio-economic prominence of the Suthar elite in Bulsar.

Wealth was unequally distributed among Suthars; the 425 households differed considerably economically. Suthars themselves distinguished between four economic categories:

I. 40-50 'well-to-do' households
II. 140-150 'not-rich, not-poor' households
III. 200 households which found it 'difficult to pull on'
IV. 10-20 'poor' households

The present research concentrated on the extremes of the stratification. The telephone directory confirmed the information: 44 connections belonged to 38 households.[4] The most prosperous of these 38 families were contractors and the two families selling tractors and manufacturing agricultural implements. The economic top also included two families with furniture workshops, a family owning a large general store, a computer specialist and two ex-manufacturers of bobbins.

'Neither rich, nor poor' Suthars owned small workshops, like a garage, photo-studios and general shops. Some of them belonged to the 38 families with telephones. Many of them were government servants, railway personnel, or employees of private companies like Atul Products and its sister concerns. Extra earnings from advisory jobs and administrative work supplemented their stable incomes. They were part of the growing middle class of Bulsar. They had their own houses in 'Suthar streets', built around 1940 outside the old town, or occupied apartments in the new buildings of the town.

Those who 'found it difficult to pull on' could best be described as 'skilled workers', like carpenters, fitters, turners, welders, or electricians. They earned between Rs. 750 and 900 a month. Other

Suthars employed them, or they served as skilled workers and supervisors in small-scale factories located along the roads outside Bulsar and at Gundlav and Vapi industrial estates. They stayed in the old and poor areas of the town in rented houses or in their own, old and dilapidated homes.

Suthar friends differentiated between those 'who find it difficult to pull on' and households which are really 'poor'. I found it difficult to draw a sharp line between both categories. Certainly, eight poor widows' households could be distinguished from other poor households. Quality, pay and permanency of work, and irregularity of income, distinguished best between the 'difficult to pull on' and 'poor' households:

Case 1

Three brothers, staying in three separate rented houses made of wood, bricks and iron sheets, exemplify 'poor' Suthars. Their grandfather lived in Segvi, where he was employed by the grandfather of the Panchals.

Their father came to Bulsar in the 1930s. In 1940 he rented the three houses which were located in one compound outside the centre of the town, where many Suthars settled down in the 1930s and 1940s. He worked in a large furniture workshop owned by a Suthar, who also came from Segvi. One of his brothers was an employee of a bobbin factory which was founded in 1945; the other expired at an early age.

The youngest of the three brothers earned a living by transporting goods with a hand cart for other Suthars, like owners of furniture workshops. His wife was a servant in a Bania household. They had two small daughters.

The second brother worked for more than 16 hours a day, seven days in the week. He was a servant in a restaurant from 5.30 in the morning till 7 o'clock in the evening. From 8 to 11 at night he sold peanuts in front of a cinema theatre. His two sons were better off. One was a civil engineer, employed in the government department in-charge of the construction of a dam in a nearby region. He lived in a small town to the south of Bulsar, his wife worked in a bank. The other son was an employee in a factory at Vapi.

The eldest brother, who was 50 years of age, did all kinds of carpentry work. Sometimes he made tables and chairs and he was occasionally asked to make frames of doors and windows. He had two daughters and a son. His eldest daughter, who ran the household, worked in an embroidery shop. The son was an attendant in a general store.

Case 2

In this example, the householder used to make harmoniums like his father. His name was Petiwalla because *Peti* is the colloquial word for harmonium. He was born in 1920 in the village of Segvi. His father, married to a sister of the Panchals from Segvi, came to Bulsar to make harmoniums. It was unknown how he learned the craft. Petiwala started as a carpenter in a furniture workshop in Bulsar. A few years later he joined his father in making harmoniums. Petiwala's only brother was a carpenter in the railways. His son lived in Bulsar's major slum area, Shapurji Nagar, where he tried to make a living as a carpenter.

Since the 1970s Petiwala resided in a shed. He lived together with his wife; a 42-year-old daughter, who was a widow and a mother of a small child; and a mentally retarded daughter. His son expired.

The shed was furnished with junk; it had no water connection and it was not rain-proof. It was the property of one of the richest Anavil contractors in Bulsar, who wanted them to vacate the place. Petiwala and his family shifted to the present site from a house in the compound of a bobbin factory. They had to leave because the Suthar owners needed the space. Petiwala's household lived from the income of the widow. She was a factory worker at Gundlav Industrial Estate. She earned about Rs. 300 a month, which is too little to live on.

The Suthars in above two examples were all from the village Segvi. In the 1930s and 1940s Segvi Suthars all settled down in the same area when they came to Bulsar. The poverty of Suthars in Cases 1 and 2 did not mean that poor Suthars descended from certain villages, like Segvi. The examples show the economic differentiation among Suthars who originated from the same native village. It is tempting to account for the differentiation among Suthars by pointing to social or economic inequalities already existing decades ago. For instance, the grandfathers and fathers in the above examples were employed by caste fellows in Segvi or in Bulsar. The economic position of their employers enabled their offspring to be more educated, to get better jobs, or contributed to their success as entrepreneurs. The histories of prosperous Suthars also show fathers or grandfathers employed by other Suthars. For instance, the father of the most wealthy furniture maker in Bulsar, and the father of the three brothers in Case 1 both came from Segvi and were both employees in the same furniture workshop in Bulsar. The former started his own business in the 1940s, the latter remained an employee in the workshop.

Case 1 shows that individual variables explain why some families prospered, and others remained or became poor. The variables are of two types. The first pertains to personal attributes like intellectual capacity, craftsmanship, entrepreneurial abilities, and other psychological characteristics. The second type of individual variables I call 'vicissitudes of life', like illness, death, and other disasters which are beyond human control.[5] In a society without social security provided by the state, they can ruin families and marginalize them within one generation. Petiwala and his family are an example. His father expired when he was young. He had been sickly during his whole life and his eyes were weak. His brother had been unable to help him. He lost his only son; his son-in-law expired; and his second daughter was mentally retarded. In other words, there was nobody to fall back upon.

Social inequality between the Suthar elite and Banias, Anavils and Parsis, who belonged to the social and economic establishment of Bulsar in the 1970s, remained (Streefkerk, 1985: 104). For instance, Suthars were not represented in the Municipal Council in those years. None of them achieved membership in the Rotary Club, the pre-eminently elite association in Bulsar. They were, however, well represented in the Lions Club, which was the club for the new elite of the town.

Between 1900 and 1990 Suthars lost their monopoly over building construction and the first generation of industrial entrepreneurs vanished. The older generation did not benefit from the chances offered by the economic expansion during the last decade, like the Jeepwalas and Panchals. In the social and political life of the town they remained to play a minor role. In 1990 they were still not represented in the Municipal Council. In other elite bodies, like the Rotary Club,

Suthars became members during the 1970s and 1980s. The Lions Club had been presided by a Suthar for many years in the 1990s.

SUTHAR STATUS

Attempts to enhance social esteem by claiming a higher ritual status accompanied economic progress among Suthars since 1900. This process of Sanskritization included adopting modes of behaviour, norms, values and rituals of the powerful and those which are considered characteristic of a higher 'twice-born' caste. That is, a *jati* said to belong to a top first-order division such as Brahmin, Kshatriya or Vaishya. To validate claims for higher ritual status claims have to be supported by secular attributes of wealth and power. The process of collective improvement of ritual status and enhancement of social esteem is not a recent phenomenon. Indian social history can be understood as a permanent process of groups adjusting ritual status to their material strength and political power. Or, as a history of people who emulate the lifestyle of their superiors. The gradual incorporation of tribals into the 'higher' Hindu social order in south Gujarat is an example of such a process.

Claims for higher ritual status of the artisans are not new. Mandelbaum (1970: 459) quotes accounts hinting at these claims in the seventeenth century, and at the beginning of the nineteenth century. Saberwal (1976: 110) writes that from Ceylon in the south to Punjab in the north, during the late nineteenth and twentieth centuries, artisan communities celebrated the great importance of their deity Vishwakarma, the Lord of Craftsmanship. He is Brahma's craftsman, builder and architect of the heavenly realm, said to be of Brahmin descent.[6] Saberwal calls it one of the few caste mobility movements which took a more or less parallel course throughout the subcontinent.

The date of the first claims for higher ritual status among Bulsar Suthars are unknown, but their temple, dedicated to the lord Vishwakarma, is at least 120 years old. The administration of a temple with a Brahmin priest is a direct means to enhance ritual status. In south India, carpenters together with goldmiths, coppermiths, masons, and blacksmiths, claim to be Brahmins of a special kind, descended from Vishwakarma (Mandelbaum, 1970: 458). In Bulsar, Suthars said they were strict vegetarians. Some of them wore the sacred thread, symbolizing their 'twice-born' status. They maintained that a certain amount of dowry was not uncommon. The establishment of the Panchal Pragati Mandal in 1948 in Bulsar was another indication of Suthar claims for higher status. The word Panchal in the name of the organization and as surname of some Suthars in Bulsar expressed the same. In south India the artisan *jatis* appropriated the common title Panchalla; *panch* means five, the number of groups of artisans which claimed to be Brahmins. In Bulsar, Suthars explained the origin of the name Panchal in the same way. Nevertheless, only Suthars and Luhars were permitted to become members of the organization. Sonis (goldsmith), Kansaras (braziers) and Kumbhars (potters) were not welcome, and they had their own associations.

In 1983 the administration of the Vishwakarma Temple and Panchal Pragati Mandal were brought together into one organization: Panchal Sewa Samaj. The reason to unite the two organizations was efficiency; the same people were active in the two organizations. The disappearance of the older generation of prominent Suthars, who had been active in the Panchal Pragati Mandal, might be another reason. The younger generation of leading Suthars, like an architect, a furniture maker and the owner of a large general store, administered the organization. Like the former Mandal, the Samaj supports widows, helps poor Suthar students to buy books, and offers sewing and computer courses, which are conducted in the new Vishwakarma Hall.

The construction of the Vishwakarma Hall in 1988 was another step towards organizational strength. The large three-storied building accommodated the shrine of Vishwakarma. It replaced the old, much smaller temple building. The construction of the building had been financed by a donation of a rich Suthar, who had been a contractor. The building was located in the old part of the town; its site also belonged to Suthars. The shrine of Vishwakarma stood in the hall on the groundfloor. Personal computers and printers filled one of its rooms on the first floor. The room was rented by a Suthar who processed information and administration on behalf of Atul and enterprises located at Gundlav, Vapi, and in and around the town.

In 1990, by the organization of collective marriage ceremonies and the presentation of potential brides and grooms Suthars demonstrated internal unity, mutual concern and organizational power. The Panchal

Sewa Samaj organized the two annual events in Bulsar. The total expenses of the festivities amounted to Rs. 50,000; Rs. 40,000 was spent on food. An entrance fee of Rs. 75 per person covered the expenses. Each Suthar household in Bulsar received one ticket free of charge. Each family of the seven couples to be married during the ceremony obtained, 25 tickets, 80 tickets were distributed among the volunteers who helped to organize the festivities.

Guests came from Bulsar and from other places in south Gujarat. They arrived on scooters and motor bikes, in private cars and in rented buses. Among the guests were representatives of Suthar organizations in Mumbai, Surat, Baroda and Ahmedabad and smaller towns in south Gujarat. During the meeting in 1990 seven Suthar couples were married. Seven Brahmin priests conducted the ceremonies and the couples received all kinds of practical gifts from the Samaj.

Late in the afternoon 25 young marriageable Suthar men and women, almost all inabitants of distant villages, presented themselves to the visitors. Their parents or other family members had given their names to the Samaj. They sat on the stage in two rows, the men in the first, and the women in the second row. While a member of the board of the organization read out the name, native place, age, education and source of income, the candidate walked to the front of the stage. Guests who wanted to arrange a marriage between their son or daughter and one of the candidates could contact the Samaj after the ceremony.

The collective marriage ceremony and the presentation of marriageable candidates signified the importance of maintaining the principles of arranged marriages and caste endogamy among Suthars. Second, the ceremony involved families who were not well-off. Suthars explicitly stated that it was meant for people who could not afford a lavish wedding. They were less outspoken about Suthars who participated in the presentation, though background and native place of the candidates suggested they were not from prosperous families either. Suthars validated their claims for a superior ritual status by enabling less well-off caste members to marry their children according to expensive Brahmin ideals. At the same time they honoured the idea that the 'community' cared for its unfortunate members. Finally, the festivities emphasized unity among Suthars despite considerable economic differences. They furthermore contributed to an identity that exceeded local level. Representatives of other Suthar associations addressed the meeting and referred to their common origin: 'Long ago Lord Brahma ordered Vishwakarma to create the world, Suthars must do it now, they are Vishwakarma's children'.[7]

CONCLUSION

Bulsar Suthars became urban residents during the first half of twentieth century. This process implied occupational diversification and economic differentiation. The gradual deviation from traditional skills and migration from native villages enabled upward economic mobility. Occupations of wealthy Suthars, such as contractor, architect, manufacturer of modern furniture, or heavy agricultural implements, emanated from their traditional occupation in 1990. The most prosperous Suthars were not the most wealthy inhabitants of Bulsar, but they certainly were part of the economic elite of the town. Many Suthars belonged to the town's ascending middle class. They owned stores and small workshops, were government servants, railway personnel or employees of private companies. Their occupations developed out of their ancestral craft too.

The heads of almost half of the Suthar households earned a living as carpenters, fitters, turners, welders and the like. Their households were at the lower end of the economic stratification. The poorest among them lacked a regular source of income; they were self-employed or casual labourers. Some of them had to combine a poorly paid regular jobs with other sporadic earnings. Women of these poor families contributed to the income of their households by working as domestic servants of well-to-do families.

The rise to political prominence of a Suthar who became the chairman of the municipal council accompanied economic mobility among Suthars around 1950. But he did not set a trend; between 1960 and 1990 Suthars did not play an important role in the politics of the municipality or in the wider political arena. But they they took part in 'social work' and offered donations. They thus participated in projects which symbolized increased welfare in, and prestige of the town. Suthars satisfied their quest for more social esteem by strengthening their ritual status. This tendency intensified during the second half of the 1980s. Suthars built a large new temple and organized the first collective marriage ceremonies.

Members of the metropolitain middle classes[8] in cities like Mumbai, Delhi and Kolkata are ambivalent about caste, according to Beteille (1996: 152).[9] He adds that it is difficult to generalize because of size and diversity of this upper stratum (Beteille: 152). Well-to-do inhabitants of Gujarati cities confirm the impossibility of generalizing. In a big Gujarati city like Baroda, with about 1.1 million inhabitants in the 1990s, prosperous Prajapatis[10] (Kumbhars) and Sonis were members of caste associations which organized group marriages, caste welfare activities, and published directories, caste journals and books (Engelshoven, 1993: 56-108).

Suthar members of the Bulsar middle class are not ambivalent about caste as well. Yet, some aspects of their lifestyle did not differ from that of the Mumbai or Delhi middle classes. Brothers and sisters of the Suthars in Bulsar commuted between the town and Mumbai or lived and worked in Delhi or Kolkata. In 1990 Suthar children and sometimes even their parents read the periodical *India Today*, listened to Sting and Phil Collins, and enjoyed Michael Jackson like their metropolitan counterparts.[11]

Caste is among the determinants of economic mobility and the formation of upper and lower classses. In south Gujarat, Anavil Brahmins were among the first to monopolize new educational facilities and occupations before 1900. Suthars profited from economic changes later on. Kolis and Dhodias recently captured economic possibilities in the villages and exploited administrative and political opportunities. What is noteworthy is not so much people's ability to take advantage of new opportunities but their success as caste groups, such as Anavils, Suthars, Kolis or Dhodias. When people failed it was, and still is, because they belonged to underprivileged groups, like Naikas or Dublas, which were unable to participate. The seizure of scarce resources, administrative influence and political power happened within the moral order and structural framework of caste. It developed into an institution through with groups compete with each other for power and resources.[12]

The emergence of huge caste groups, or *horizontal stretch* (Srinivas, 1979: 241), is a contemporary expression of the caste structure. Caste associations are a concrete manifestation of this tendency. They are an urban phenomena, at least in western India. The earliest associations were formed in Mumbai in the middle of the nineteenth century by migrants belonging to urban upper castes from Gujarat. Caste associations then spread to towns in Gujarat and among all castes. After Independence rural and lower castes were the last to form associations. Some of the associations, like the Gujarat Kshatriya Sabha, adopted political functions after the establishment of a democratic polity after 1947. Most associations, like the Suthar Association in Bulsar, continued to retain their non-political character (Shah, 1982: 28, 29) and tried to attain a higher position in the caste hierarchy (Engelshoven 1993: 141).

In Bulsar people complained that 'we, middle class people, suffer most from inflation because *we* have to maintain our lifestyle and customs against rising prices; poor people don't have these problems'. It was a sign of an emerging class consciouness among the middle class residents of the town. The developments among the Suthars during the 1980s, however, reveal a much stronger tendency. Economic mobility and prosperity among them was expressed by heightened caste consciousness.[13] It was shared also by Suthars whose poor material conditions were similar to those of the of the bulk of the population of the town. The identification with their caste might be even more important for them than for more well-to-do Suthars. It enabled them to consider others, whether rich or poor, as socially inferior.

NOTES

1. Suthars, like Kumbhars traditionally belonged to the so-called 'service' castes, whose members were paid in kind (*avat*) for their services rendered to their 'patrons', the landowners.
2. Streefkerk (1985: 68-105) provides a detailed analysis of the transition from handicraft to industrial production.
3. Moulik and Moulik (1989: 31) show the close link between increased irrigation and tractorization in Gujarat. In 1961 the total number of tractors was 2,000, in 1972 it was 14,400 and in 1982, the number was 28,100.
4. Occupations of Bulsar Suthars with a telephone (1988)

Occupation	*Numbers*
Owners of small workshops	11
Contractors, architects, interior decorators	6
Furniture makers	4
Owners of stores	4

Ex-bobbin manufacturers	4
Tractor dealers, etc.	2
Professionals	2
Service	2
Lodge owner	1
Unknown	3
Total	39

5. See, for example, Willem van Schendel (1981: 279) about 'nature and chance' as causes for short-term or long-term rise and fall of certain groups or even single families within the peasantry.
6. The difference between popular ideas and sacred scriptures appears from these quotes and Basham's observation that 'there is no clearly defined creator-god in the main body of the *Rgveda.* By the end of the Rgvedic period (probably 1000 BC), however, such a god had developed.... This god was Prajapati, 'the Lord of Beings', later called Brahma, the masculine form of the neuter Brahman (Basham, 1959: 240).
7. Ibid.
8. Beteille's urban middle class includes intelligentsia, professionals, service class, schoolteachers, clerks, 'other' white-collar workers, managers and higher professionals (1996: 151).
9. This ambivalence is very marked among judges, lawyers, journalists and academics (Beteille, 1996: 152). Saberwal (1979: 251) notes the tendency among Indian sociologists to document the decline of caste because they experienced 'opportunity and mobility' in their own lives and therefore focussed on similar situations of mobility and change elsewhere. He concludes his *Mobile Man* (1976: 225 and 231) with the observation that the caste hierarchy in Punjab has softened further during the last decades and that the caste system, its religious supports and caste solidarity declined in the town he studied.
10. In 1992, the chairman of the Municipal Council of Vadodara was a Prajapati.
11. Sujata Patel (2003: 5, 6) writes that contemporary urban forms of culture in Mumbai appear as large mosaic ethnic products and spectacles like Ganpati festivals and Michael Jackson shows.
12. Because cooperation and mutual dependence between different caste groups traditionally characterized the caste system in the villages, competition between caste groups is a deviation of traditional caste in India (Srinivas, 1979: 242).
13. The Mudaliyar (weaver) caste in the Tamil Nadu town of Tiruchendu exhibit similar trends. Fuller (1996: 15) writes that Mudaliyars show how 'thriving mercantile capitalism can reinforce . . . cultural distinctiveness among castes' and how they mobilize a united front.

CHAPTER 5

Workers in 1998: Casualization and Feminization

The decline of state control over economic life marks Indian political economy since the mid-1980s. Until the 1970s, the Indian political economy was state capitalist. The government controlled industrial production and protected it against foreign competition. The state shared control of the industrial economy with huge privately owned industrial houses. In 1991, the central government issued a New Industrial Policy Statement, abolishing the complex system of obtaining official permits in order to start and expand industrial enterprises. The new policy also announced the reform of state-owned industrial production by allowing private investment in fields earlier considered public domain, or private participation in public ventures. Finally, but no less important, the new policy encouraged foreign investments and continued to remove restrictions on imports. With these measures, the Indian government aimed to foster greater internal and external industrial competition and thus improve industrial efficiency, productivity, and modernization of industrial technology (Mani, 1995). South Gujarat's industrialized west coast exemplifies the changing political economy of India.

The social consequences of liberalization have been analysed by Panini (1995 and 1996). He distinguishes short-term trends and long-term effects. In the long run, liberalization may dissolve caste-based distinctions because enhanced productivity will generate more employment and so diminish appeals to traditional loyalties such as caste in securing jobs (Panini, 1996: 60). In the short run, however, liberalization may exacerbate inter-caste conflicts and sharpen caste identities because market forces favour those who are well endowed with skills and resources. These are members of the upper castes, the professionally-oriented capitalist class in cities and towns, and the dominant peasant castes in rural areas (Panini, 1996: 61). Others maintain that the economic and social effects of liberating Indian economy from government controls, and especially the deregulation of industrial production, will result in the casualization of industrial labour. More competition, greater efficiency, and introduction of new technologies will lead to reducing the costs of labour and facilitate elimination of excess workers. Reductions in the labour force and non-permanent employment of cheap labour will be the result (Mani, 1995; Noronha, 1996; Shah and Gandhi, 1998).

This chapter describes the changes in size and features of the local industrial labour force during the relevant 30 years and discusses whether these changes can be the result of the recent liberalization of the Indian economy.

THE INDUSTRIAL WORK FORCE IN BULSAR

The locations of the major industrial sites in the Bulsar region did not change. One of these is still Bulsar town and its immediate surroundings, the other is the huge industrial plant of Atul-Atic, which is located 7 km south of Bulsar town. The town and its immediate surroundings include several concentrations of industrial enterprises located along the roads leading to the town, along the NH 8, near the banks of the Auranga River, and in the nearby industrial estate of Gundlav.

In the 1970s there were no reliable records on the number of workshops, factories, and workers in the immediate surroundings of Bulsar town. The estimate of approximately 2,500 workers in 1974 was based on my visits to the region and on tallying almost all its local industrial establishments and their workers (Chapter 2). One researcher and his assistant could easily survey the local industrial situation; this is no longer the case. At present, the factories inspector keeps records of the number of registered factories and workers in the Bulsar region.

His cramped office consists of a few small rooms on the second floor of a building in the old bazaar of the town. Unlike the staff of factories I visited, the inspector and his personnel have to do without modern administrative facilities like personal computer, fax, and a so-called National Subscriber Dialing telephone connection. Calls outside Bulsar telephone district have to be made downstairs, in the shop of KK Biscuits, in one of the many privately owned STD telephone booths.

According to the inspector, there are 265 registered industrial enterprises located in Bulsar town and its immediate surroundings, including the industrial estate of Gundlav. Officially, these enterprises employ a total number of 9,603 workers, which is an average of 36 workers per factory. The factories included in the count are registered industrial establishments as established in the Factories Act of 1948.

The Act's definition of a 'factory' is still the point of departure for other sections of the labour legislation such as the Payment of Bonus Act. These require various benefits to workers employed for an uninterrupted period of 240 days.

To save expenses on workers, construction, and equipment, owners continued to be permanently occupied in keeping their enterprises and workers outside the purview of this Act. Their methods have not changed since the 1970s:

Owners officially employed fewer than 10 workers by splitting up their firms; they regularly closed sections and recommenced them again under different names; by laying off workers and reinstating them after some time; or by keeping two accounts, one meant for officials and the other for internal use; and by keeping those who are appointed to supervise them satisfied, i.e. the factories inspector and his staff.

As a result, it is impossible to know the actual number of industrial establishments and workers in the Bulsar region from official statistics. Many workers employed in these industrial firms are not included in the tally. The available figures only include registered industrial enterprises. They do not take into account many firms that fall outside the definition of the Factories Act. In order to collect information about the number of industrial workers in the Bulsar region, I also visited the spacious and well-equipped office of the Bulsar Association of Small Scale Industries.

The president of the Association estimated that there were 1,200 enterprises in the Bulsar region. These include industrial establishments with a capital investment not exceeding Rs. 1 crore. Assuming that each establishment employs on average 12 persons, the president calculated that these 1,200 small enterprises would together employ a total of 14,400 persons.

However, in the end, he had to admit that it was very difficult to determine the real numbers: 'Actually nobody knows the exact figures, there are plenty of units with fewer than ten labourers and even I don't know many of them.'

The only conclusion the official figures and those of the Association allow is that the absolute number of industrial workers in Bulsar town and its immediate surroundings increased enormously during the 1980s and 1990s. The increase occurred mainly between 1985 and 1990 according to owners and officials.

The second concentration of industrial activity in the Bulsar region remained the huge chemical plant of Atul-Atic located 7 km south of Bulsar. It consists of five large enterprises that produce dyes, intermediates, basic chemicals, drugs, and pesticides. The company has local importance in the region. The Lalbhais, textile magnates from Ahmedabad, founded the plant in 1952. It was the first industrial establishment in the southern part of south Gujarat. In the late 1960s and early 1970s, its presence encouraged the formation of a series of small workshops in Bulsar and its immediate environs, which manufactured chemical dyestuffs and intermediates, predominantly sold to Atul-Atic.

In the 1970s the plant employed 4,400 workers. Many hailed from villages located in the different sub-districts of Bulsar (Kapadia and Pillai, 1972). Today, Atul-Atic employs about 9,500 workers. Many of them still live in local villages. It is common knowledge in Bulsar that 'Atul-Atic is in serious trouble.' The president of one of its companies confirms the problems. They are the clearest local manifestation of the central policy to liberate industrial production. Atul-Atic has to face foreign competitors now from China, Turkey, Thailand, and Malaysia. One of the remedies was to update the company's labour-intensive technology and automate parts of its production processes. Consequently, hundreds of workers became redundant and were pensioned off.

The president did not lose his optimism. He still recognized the local function of Atul-Atic, which 'has been important to the development of this area and is the seed and catalyst of a region which spans 20 km'. He concluded by saying that 'an elephant, however weak it may become, will never become a buffalo but will always remain an elephant'. By this he meant that Atul-Atic would remain a giant despite the unfavourable developments.

The number of workers in these two industrial concentrations in the Bulsar region has increased substantially over the past 30 years. Unlike the bulk[1] of workers at Vapi industrial estate, workers in the

Bulsar region are still of local origin. This continuity does not mean that labour relations remained the same in Bulsar and its immediate surroundings.

TEMPERWALI AND CONTRACT WORKERS

The distinction between permanent and temporary workers characterized the local industrial work force of the Bulsar region in the 1970s. The owners' permanent efforts to evade the labour acts and the carelessness of officers who were supposed to enforce compliance resulted in a predominance of temporary workers

At the end of the 1990s the distinction between permanent and temporary workers was still important in the region. Owners, workers, and officials constantly differentiated between the two categories, and the distinction has become part of their language. Temporary workers, or 'temperwali' as they refer to themselves, generally performed the unskilled jobs, which include the strenuous activities like loading and unloading, feeding machines, packing finished products, and cleaning. Their maximum pay did not exceed the official daily minimum wage of Rs. 63 for 8 hours in 1998. Furthermore, the temperwali did not get any fringe benefits and could be easily dismissed.

Thus, the difference between temperwali and permanent workers is that unlike temperwali, permanent workers are paid more; their employers contribute to their provident fund (pension); they receive benefits like bonuses and paid leaves; and they are not regularly laid off. Generally, they are technically more skilled or experienced and are considered indispensable and more loyal. They are found in both small and large factories, their jobs are characterized by more than a rudimentary division of labour, and they generally use more complex technology, such as in the engineering industry. Permanent workers earn at least the official minimum wage. Skilled permanent workers in engineering, sophisticated plastics, or pharmaceuticals are paid a salary of Rs. 4,000-5,000 per month plus benefits. Highly skilled workers are paid even more. Being a temperwali, however, does not mean a worker is temporarily employed by the same company forever. Some labourers working in the same factory for years received their benefits, and their employer contributed to their provident fund after an initial period of temporary labour. However, others employed by the same concern for a long time, never received such emoluments.

Sun Toys, a successful engineering factory manufacturing small electrical motors for toys, illustrates wage differences and different modes of employment. Since 1971, the factory has been located along one of the roads leading out of Bulsar. The motors are sold in India and for the past few years the owner has tried to export them to the USA and Japan. In the entrance hall there is a big and brightly coloured statue of Ganpati (Ganesh). The god is illuminated by strings of small electrical bulbs. A few garlands lie over his fat belly. A painted disk, also decorated with bulbs of different colours, revolves behind his elephant head. It is driven by an electrical motor made by the factory.

When I enter the workplace I feel that I am back in the 1970s again. Its machinery, mainly powered lathes and hand presses, is old-fashioned and dates back to those years. 'Indeed, technically there has been little change since 1970, mechanization is too expensive and I will never be able to recover my expenses', the owner explains.

He employs about 70 workers, of which 30 are in permanent service. Two highly skilled die-makers receive Rs. 8,000 per month, or Rs. 307 per day. Several skilled workers such as lathe operators earn Rs. 4,000 per month or Rs. 153 per day. The other less experienced or less skilled permanent workers get a daily wage between Rs. 70 and 100.

Forty workers are temperwali who don't receive benefits and are regularly laid off. Twenty of them are young men performing manual labour, like powering the simple and outdated hand presses, or carrying raw material and unfinished parts from one machine to another or from one section of the factory building to the other.

The other 20 workers are young women. Sitting behind a long table in a separate room, they do the 'nimble finger work'. They assemble the different parts of the small motors, test the electrical parts, and pack them. They are temporarily employed, earning Rs. 50 per day. The two older women who supervise them are permanently employed with a daily wage of about Rs. 70.

A major change that has occurred in recent years is that more and more workers are employed through officially recognized contractors. Alongside the distinction between temperwali and permanent workers, the distinction between 'workers employed by contractors' and 'workers employed by the company' has come into being. This new distinction is almost the same as the earlier one, which is still used by workers and owners. Workers often mix the two concepts; sometimes they refer to themselves as temperwali even though they are employed as contract workers.

What has happened can best be understood as the formalization of an unofficial distinction. This took place as a result of the Contract Labour Act (1970). The Act enables owners to recruit and employ workers through labour contractors. Workers are hired and paid by a contractor and not by the company. To become a labour contractor, a license is needed. The Assistant Commissioner of Labour in Bulsar issues the license which must be renewed annually for Rs. 37.50 per license, a security deposit of Rs. 2,700, and an additional Rs. 1,000 to satisfy the Commissioner. A license allows the contractor to employ 30 workers per company. He earns Rs. 3 per day for each worker, which is paid by the company he mediates for. The contractor pays workers the official minimum wage or less. Once a month the contractor claims his fees and expenses from the company, which the company remits to his account.

Contractors must also pay workers various benefits after they have employed the workers for a certain length of time; some of them do, but others do not. They can easily evade the rules by terminating the contract before the period ends. For instance, a contractor in Bulsar ended the contract of almost 50 workers during 1997 by claiming that he was not satisfied with them. In other cases, contracts were terminated because the management complained about the attendance or job performance of the contract workers. Fake bookkeeping is another method: contractors keep records detailing the daily minimum wages and emoluments they paid to the contract workers they employ for the companies they mediate for. Actually, the contractors keep the difference between what they really pay the workers and the money reimbursed by the company. In 1998 alone there were about eight such labour contractors in the town of Bulsar and its environs.

Almost all large factories in need of unskilled labour employ contract workers for the heavy work. They do so by using different contractors for different departments like packing, carting, loading, and unloading. Of the 9,500 workers employed in Atul-Atic, 3,000 are contract workers. The drug manufacturing company in the vicinity of the village of Lalgam employs 300 people, of which 150 are contract workers. A large chemical factory at Gundlav estate with about 100 permanent workers employs another 200 people through 6 contractors. Its total workforce thus far exceeds the average of 11 workers per registered factory at the estate. This average was calculated from figures collected by the factories inspector: at Gundlav he counted 102 factories with a total of 1,100 workers in 1998.

Owners and managers prefer contract labour because it enables them to be 'flexible' and to save money. They can more easily adapt their workforce to the economic fluctuations dictated by market and climate. In other words, whenever necessary they can reduce the size of their workforce without provoking union leaders and without the need to circumvent the often expensive and always irritating official 'harassment'. They also employ contract workers because it shifts the burden of controlling workers to contractors. To be able to dismiss unskilled labour when no longer needed or to get rid of those who do not work well or create problems, managers simply tell the contractors that they no longer want them. Furthermore, owners and managers are no longer employers of a large part of their workforce. In this way they are unaffected by the constant threat of union leaders for whom activism is the means to livelihood. For the union leaders a strike means more income, because each settlement results in the owner paying higher wages, and the leaders receive an agreed-upon percentage of the increments.

Workers do not like to be contract workers, but they have no choice because they are in need of work. Those in search of jobs tell the watchman at the factory gate that they want work. He sends them to Bulsar to contractors who work for their factory. It is not always easy to get a contract. For instance, workers complain that to get a contract, *lagvag* (influence) is required. Some contractors distribute jobs only after mediation by local politicians. Other complaints pertain to the payment of wages. Workers say that they do not get paid in time, while some report they have not received anything at all.

The most crucial danger of being employed as a contract worker is the loss of albeit limited shelter. Temperwali who are dismissed temporarily by the owner to evade being subject to restrictive legislation can hope to be reinstated again after some time. Contractors often do not give new contracts after having terminated old ones. Furthermore, even without receiving benefits, being employed directly by the owner provides some protection. Unlike contractors, owners give small loans when there is an emergency. Temporary workers also hope that they will ultimately become permanent. For contract workers this is not a realistic possibility. Or, as one of them said: 'If I ask my supervisor about these things I will be removed.'

Temperwali are economically and socially 'less casual' than contract workers, who represent the most recent tendency in the evolution of local industrial relations. Despite differences, they can both be classified as casual industrial labour. The insecurity of their tenure, absence of benefits, and paucity of wages put both groups in the same category. Furthermore, both are beyond the reach of legislation. Thus they are ignored by officials and union leaders, who view labour laws as the basis for mediation between capital and labour. The increase in casual labour in the local industrial workforce has been a major change over the last 30 years. At present, more than 60 per cent of the local industrial workforce is either temperwali or contract workers.

MUKADAMS AND CONTRACTORS

There have always been jobbers or mediators (*mukadams*) between capital and labour in India. Breman shows how they act in south Gujarat's agricultural sector. He describes them as brokers who operate in the context of seasonal migration from, within, and into south Gujarat. These brokers are 'bosses of the work gang (they) ... recruited'. They have the same origins as the workers but act under the employer's orders. *Mukadams* advance money obtained from employers to villagers during the rainy season when they lack income (Breman, 1996: 93). *Mukadams* from south Gujarat recruit workers to work in the salt pans on the outskirts of Mumbai or in brickyards elsewhere in south Gujarat. Khandeshi *mukadams* supply cooperative sugar mills in the plains of south Gujarat with cane-cutters that were recruited from their villages in the Khandesh (Breman, 1978).

Mukadams were common in large industrial centres like Mumbai. They maintained a powerful grip on workers through their personal contacts. This group had no role in the early industrialization of Bulsar and its sub-district because close contacts between owners and workers made *mukadams* unnecessary as a means of labour control during this period. Usually owners recruited workers from their immediate social and geographic environs, or through workers already employed in their factories. Patronage and personal dependencies characterized incipient industrial relations in the small factories. Being proprietors, owners considered the factory their domain and the workers to be 'their' labourers (Chapter 3).

In 1998 there were no *mukadams* in the industrial companies of Bulsar and its immediate surroundings. The mediators who supplied workers to factories in the Bulsar region were different from *mukadams* because they did not contract seasonal workers, nor did they supervise the workers they supplied. These labour contractors certainly did not belong to the social milieu of the workers they employed. They were part of the emerging middle class of Bulsar which characterized the town's class structure in the 1990s. The middle class comprised several levels, including managers, professionals, small-scale industrialists, small businessmen, shop owners, government personnel, and employees of private firms.

Lad, a member of the middle class, had a great-grandfather who was a potter (Kumbhar) and a grandfather who was a Carpenter. I met his father in his workshop on the outskirts of Bulsar town in 1971. He manufactured small wooden parts used in printing textiles. Lad inherited the workshop from his father. Eight workers continued to produce the same wooden items with the same instruments in the same workshop at the same location.

He also owns the firm Prajapati Traders, which he started in the early 1990s. Through this firm he runs his contracting business. A *jati bhai* contractor in Vapi advised him to start a contracting firm in Bulsar because a manager of a Bulsar factory went to a Vapi contractor in search of contract labour.

Lad is an example of those artisans in Bulsar, like other Kumbhars, Suthars, and Luhars, who succeeded socially and economically. Lad employs about 100 workers in a factory at the industrial estate of Gundlav outside Bulsar on four different licenses. He states, 'I don't visit workers, they come to me. They arrive from villages as far as 10 km from here (Bulsar).' Twice a week Lad drives his scooter to the industrial estate to visit the human resource manager of the chemical company that he supplies with labour.

The absence of jobbers in the 1970s can be understood, but how can the emergence of labour contractors in the 1990s be explained?

Jobbers are a manifestation of advanced capitalist industrial production. At the end of 1980s and in the 1990s, the size and number of factories increased and their organization changed. Industrial enterprises with more than 100 workers were no longer an exception, and neither was the separation between ownership and management. In several companies, production and technology and labour and sales were the responsibilities of salaried experts. Some were of local origin, others outsiders. These changes hampered rather than encouraged personal contacts between workers and management; they stimulated impersonal modes of recruitment and control. Furthermore, officially approved contractors lend respectability and facilitate the practices that owners and managers have resorted to from the early 1970s onwards. These include keeping parts of the workforce in temporary service and dismissing workers no longer needed or considered troublesome. Moreover, management can shed the burden of controlling parts of the labour force and, last but not least, escape its expected social responsibilities.

BETWEEN DEPENDABILITY AND CALCULATION

Owners of smaller factories that use more complex technology, such as engineering firms, do not work through contractors: 'We don't employ contract workers, we need experienced and semi-skilled workers, and then contract workers are of no use.' Nor do owners of factories that predominantly use labourers for heavy work employ contract workers.

Shah, who owns a small factory that manufactures dyes and other chemicals, is one of them. He said, as if protesting against too much estrangement: 'We don't go by contractors, because then we don't have any base. We employ only known persons. We need confidence and that we get through recommendation. Then they don't dare to disappoint, they should have fear in their minds.'

Shah's words express that change towards objectified industrial relations is not an unambiguous development. In the 1990s the increased number and size of factories altered management structures, and more contract workers signified advanced capitalist production as well as more alienated or anonymous industrial relations. This trend is by no means linear, however. Despite their increased size, many establishments in the Bulsar region remained owner-manager firms whose owners do not work with labour contractors. Their attitudes do not differ much from factory owners in the 1970s. They still derive personal satisfaction and *ijjat* (prestige) from 'giving employment'. One of them explains that 'what gives me pride and happiness are those 100 workers whom I can give shelter and help . . . and who are dependent on me.' Or: 'I am their emergency source . . . I also see to the education of their children . . . for bright students we try to find employment in firms of friends.'

This topic, formulated in different ways, regularly recurred in my conversations with owners. For instance: 'These 150 workers give me a sort of community feeling which makes me feel happy. This gives prestige, I am an employer.' And 'I provide 100 people with a living' and (unlike trade) 'we are responsible for 100 households. In this way we build a society.'

These quotes articulate the still important ideals for local owner-managers of having ties with others, making others dependent, and being dependable.

In the course of the same conversations they were also called 'too articulate', 'after money only', and a 'nuisance'. In the 1970s the owners' discourse had been different. Then they would emphasize workers' 'backwardness', 'lack of culture', 'indulgence to drink', and 'idleness'. This changed discourse may express the owners' growing irritation with, or even fear of, workers' lack of compliance. It indicates the tendency to consider workers a burden rather than an amenity. It also signifies growing tensions between standards of personal gratification and prestige, on the one hand, and rules of economic efficiency dictated by managing factories and recent changes in industrial policy, on the other. Even the exponent of advanced capitalist production, the labour contractor, rejects too much alienation and prefers to remain within the limits of tradition: 'I only employ workers through known people. Strangers may create problems and I am responsible.'

Contradictions arise between preferences for personal contacts and ideals of dependency and standards of economic calculation or fears for workers' noncompliance. Such contradictions may be expected to be less pronounced among professional managers. The ambivalence voiced by a former managing-director of Atul-Atic, who is now director of a new pharmaceutical company, suggests that differences between salaried managers and owners are less obvious. He maintains that 'there is always the uneasy equilibrium between loyalty and pay.' The sharpest distinction may not be between owners and managers, but between generations: junior owners and experts suffer less from conflicting ideals than senior proprietors and managers. The much younger human resource manager of the same pharmaceutical company certainly does not have any doubts: 'If I were to start a factory, I would invest in machines . . . fewer people is less trouble.'

WOMEN

Women contributed substantially to the casualization of the industrial workforce in the region. My observations suggest that their numbers have increased considerably during the last few decades, but I am not able to present figures about their increased participation.

In the 1970s female workers constituted a small minority. In 1979 in my sample of 12 industrial enterprises employing a total of 185 workers, I counted only 10 women. However, in the few workshops of the still small Chain Electricals, women were already a majority. At present there are 200 girls and 75 boys. Those who have worked in this workshop for some length of time will be transferred to one of the other small workshops of Chain Electricals. This happens with two workers per month on an average. The practice has remained the same for the last 25 years.

The increase in female labour is a reflection of the fact that more enterprises need 'nimble finger' work. Most of these women are employed by Chain Electricals, India's largest producer of 'electricals', manufacturing hundreds of different types of switches, fuses, fans, bulbs, irons, tubes, electric doorbells, and other small items. At present this concern is the largest employer of female labour in the area. Hundreds of women work in dozens of workshops dispersed over villages in Bulsar taluka.

In factory halls, sometimes two stories high, women sit behind long tables with obsolete hand presses and press, assemble, control, and pack items which make up the huge assortment of products manufactured in other workshops of Chain Electricals. Educated women supervise them. They are employed permanently and receive the required benefits. The other women are kept in temporary service and paid a daily wage between Rs. 27 and 47.

These women belong to households of worker peasants. For instance, the village of Lalgam consists of numerous *faliyas*[2] (Chapter 6) inhabited by extended families belonging to different groups (Dhodia and Dubla). In almost each Dhodia *faliya* one finds one or two younger women employed in one of the Chain establishments.

In the Dubla *faliya* in almost every house there is at least one Chain woman.

Women report that they are transferred regularly from one workshop to another. For instance, during my stay two workshops were closed. Some women were laid off and others were employed again in other workshops further away from their homes. Women do not like these regular transfers because time and again they have to adjust to other staff, unknown environments and people, other routes, and, generally, to more time spent in travelling. The management of Chain tries to ease transport by running 'luxury' buses to bring women from their villages to workshops located elsewhere in the district. One of these buses collects the women from Lalwadi to drop them at places along the NH 8 and other roads and small towns where Chain workshops are located.

Daily around 7:15 in the morning 16 or 17 colourfully dressed women and a few young men gather near the tea stall at the junction of the village road and the NH 8. At 7:40 a small bus arrives with the attendant hanging outside of it and all 40 seats already occupied by women. The women from the Piruwadi part of Lalgam are squeezed inside and have to stand for at least 30 minutes before the first Chain factory is reached.

Women complain about the lack of space, duration of the journey, and traffic jams. Often the bus returns late, around 19:30 (7:30 p.m.), after dark. They have to walk for half an hour to get home, which they don't like. Walking in the village after sunset along unlit roads frightens them and impairs their reputation.

The managers of Chain Electricals prefer young unmarried women because they are inexperience and relatively more reliable than married women with children. They reason that often in-laws do not like their daughters-in-law to be employed outside the village because it sullies their reputation and the prestige of the family. Furthermore, married women cannot be depended upon to show up regularly because they have to take care of their households: husband and children, some cattle, and cultivate vegetables. In order to legitimize paying low wages and providing only temporary employment for young female employees, Chain managers use their own ideas about how women, and daughters-in-law in particular, ought to behave.

However, in the villages these ideals can be heard as well. Dhodia women, for instance, prefer to terminate external employment as soon as they are married. 'To be at home' gives prestige to their in-laws and family. Often economic necessity overrides these ideals.

For Dubla women, if they cherish 'being at home', the ideal is certainly an illusion. Chronic money shortages caused by their husbands' irregular and meagre sources of income and addiction to alcohol force them to seek outside employment. Some are happy to leave their houses and go out to work because they find peace in the factory. Their presence there releases them from quarrels and fights at home caused by the chronic drunkenness of their mates.

Others are less happy because of the behaviour of their supervisors who do not permit them to talk during work or tamper with their work appointments and pay. One woman certainly would not allow her daughters to work in Chain because of the sexual harassment she experienced from the staff. Such employment could diminish prospects of marrying them off well. Members of the Bulsar-based organization fighting the abuse of women in the district regularly receive complaints about sexual harassment in the workshops and factories in the region.

CONCLUSION

How does casualization and feminization of the local industrial labour relate to economic liberalization and the New Industrial Policy? The forced retirement of hundreds of workers employed by Atul-Atic shows that the policy did indeed affect south Gujarat. Nevertheless, it is difficult to attribute casualization of the work force directly to the retreat of the Indian State from active participation in economic life.

First, the lack of reliable statistical evidence makes it impossible to show concretely the disproportional rise of temperwali, casual, and female workers since the mid-1980s, and especially after 1991. Moreover, information that is available suggests that the largest increase in the number of factories in the region occurred before 1991, the year the central government issued the New Industrial Policy Statement.

Second, a comparison between labour conditions in the early 1970s and those in the 1990s suggests that casualization is a long-term tendency rather than a recent development. The retreat of the Indian state from its earlier active economic role did not apply to most of the industrial workers in the Bulsar region. Inadequate official data then and now suggest that for workers the State did not and still does not exist. Research in the early 1970s showed that the official underestimate of the number of workers in the small-scale industry revealed the marginal interest of the government in this field. In 1974 workers found the inspector 'indifferent'. They explained that he just 'glanced through the registration cards', and that '(w)hen he first came, he made his rounds on a bicycle, (that) now he comes on a scooter, and before long he will be coming by car' (Chapter 2). Apparently, workers did not have much reason to change their opinion after 25 years: '*Sarkar* (government) has little interest in us. The inspector regularly comes to the factory, looks into the books, gets some money, and goes.' This opinion and other statements voiced by a worker in 1998 are similar to those heard in 1974. From the early 1970s onwards, industrial production in the region has been based upon the 'invisibility' and low cost of its workers.

A direct relation between more contract workers and the liberalization of industrial production is equally difficult to establish. The Contract Labour Act dates from 1970, and from the late 1980s onwards, there has been increasing local use of contract workers because owners and managers in Bulsar region became familiar with contract labour through their connections with people at the expanding estate of Vapi. Local industrialists opened factories at the estate where labour contractors were available. The majority of the estate's labourers are migrant workers employed through contractors in Vapi. Some of the contractors are related to residents of Bulsar, so they began recruiting local labour for local factories. The employment of workers through officially recognized contractors legalizes temporary employment, which has been a major characteristic of local industrialization from the beginning.

The tendency to employ contract workers signals a different course for local industrial transition. This fact also indicates a changed work climate and altered labour relations. Such trends imply further objectification of labour relations, or greater social alienation between workers and owners or managers. Estrangement among the workers themselves seems to have become more common as well: 'Before we used to walk to the factory, have fun, and talk. Now everybody quickly disappears on their bicycles, it is all about money.' These trends did not just date from the introduction of the New Industrial Policy in 1991. Certainly, for south Gujarat, the new policy, rather than being the cause of such long-term tendencies, simply legitimizes and supports them.

NOTES

1. In the factories of Vapi, half the workers hail from other states such as Uttar Pradesh, Bihar, Maharashtra, or Kerala, whereas local worker peasants comprise a minority of about 25 per cent.
2. Hardiman (1984: 200) writes that Adivasis like Dhodias used to live in *faliyas* (small hamlets). Several *faliyas* made up a revenue unit. The villages lacked any nucleus for they were without artisans and other specialist castes.

   The Adivasi village provided a marked contrast to the so-called traditional Indian villages with their hierarchies of Brahmin priests, dominant castes, subordinated labouring castes, Bania shopkeepers, artisan castes and untouchables.

CHAPTER 6

Workers in 1998: Differentiation and Worship

In the 1970s worker-peasants made up the major part of the local industrial labour force in Bulsar region. My presence in Piruwadi enabled me to observe the permanency of this phenomenon. In 1998 the bulk of the population of Piruwadi consisted of peasant families whose members earned industrial incomes. These families owned small pieces of agricultural land that, depending on the size of the property and the household, provided with some subsistence.

My stay permitted me to see how local industrialization had influenced the lives of the villagers. This chapter contains some of these observations, beginning with Piruwadi and its village, Lalgam.

PIRUWADI

The inhabitants of Piruwadi belong administratively to the village of Lalgam. The *wadi* is located to the east of NH 8 which splits the village in two parts. Lalgam has 2,800 inhabitants who live in 600 houses, while Piruwadi has 1,620 people in 152 houses.

Dhodias constitute the largest single group. They occupy 130 houses in Piruwadi. Dublas are the second largest group, living on the fringes of the western part of the village, just across the NH 8. Ahirs (herdsmen, cattle owners) occupy 20 houses. Families of two Kukna brothers inhabit the other two houses.

Inhabitants of Piruwadi and residents of the western part of the village of Lalgam maintain that originally a few Ahir families occupied the land now called Piruwadi. All other residents of Lalgam, like Anavils, Kolis, Dhodias, and Dublas, are said be migrants who have settled in the area since 1900.

Stories told by old Dhodia men in Piruwadia have in common that their fathers or grandfathers came to Piruwadi from villages elsewhere in south Gujarat to rent some land or to work the land of Desais (Anavils).

Just across the highway the government has built two housing colonies for poor people. One, consisting of 61 houses, was erected 30 years ago to accommodate Dublas. They used to live on the banks of the Auranga River till it flooded their houses in 1968. The other colony, with 56 houses, had been built about 15 years ago. Dublas also reside there, as well as Naikas. Relatives of the Naikas live in their own dwellings further down the road.

The most opulent house in Piruwadi lies in a mango garden. The garden and house belong to an Anavil who now lives in Bulsar and is the absentee landlord of Piruwadi. He built the house in the early 1980s when he began a large mango orchard on the lands which belonged to his father. Till then the family used to live in Anavilwad in the western part of the village of Lalgam. The Kuknas, mentioned earlier, take care of the land, orchard, and house in the absence of the Anavil. The orchard is irrigated by a system of pipes connected to a tubewell owned by the Anavil. Neighbouring families are allowed to fetch drinking water from the well because villagers have to make do without piped drinking water. Others obtain drinking water from hand pumps, which have recently been installed in different parts of Piruwadi by the Panchayat administration.

There is one asphalted road in Piruwadi which ends at the centre near the primary school. It connects the *wadi* with the NH 8 and the western part of the village. In the morning and evening people come and go along this road on foot, rickshaw, and bicycle. Among this daily traffic are children who go to secondary schools in Bulsar. Some people travel on motorbikes and scooters. Now and then one of the two private cars pass by, one owned by a Dhodia and the other by an Ahir who runs a dairy farm. The road is also used by an occasional tractor, a truck driven by the Dhodia driver who stays in Piruwadi, and, of course, bullock carts and flocks of goats, which together with their Ahir herdsman leave Piruwadi in the morning to return in the evening.

Unlike many other villages in south Gujarat the village of Lalgam is a 'dry' village. Although it lies within the area of the Ukai-Kakrapur canal irrigation system, water does not reach the village; it is located at the tail-end of the system. The canals are dry, grown over with grass, shrub, and small trees.

Landowning Anavil Brahmins and the peasant caste of Kolis are the main inhabitants of the western part of Lalgam. They have their own pumps to water their lands and are able to grow the lucrative sugar cane. Paddy crops grown by the inhabitants of Piruwadi are still dependent on rains because they cannot afford to buy and install pumps. For these people the need for sources of income outside of agriculture is even more important than for residents from other villages in the area.

The distinction between landowning and land-poor or landless workers remains important, generally coinciding with the more prosperous Koli as landowners, and tribals like Dhodia, and certainly Naika, Kukna, and Dubla belonging to the land-poor groups. A Dhodia worker from Piruwadi formulated the differences between the many Koli colleagues in his factory and Dhodias as follows: 'They have more money, they come on scooters, we on bicycles.'

For owners and managers the distinction is important too. They ascribe different qualities to landless and landowning workers. They argue that landowning workers are less motivated because of the other sources of income for their households. One of them remarked: '(These) workers have no concentration, they don't have interest. They do the vegetables, some rice, some farming. They sell milk and vegetables and are not worried about their bread and butter. They work for their pocket expenses.'

Another entrepreneur emphasized: 'They don't work because they have some land, they have no food problems. They work for their entertainment and luxury. . . .'

A broader subsistence base is the reason why local owners and managers distinguish landowning workers from landless or land-poor employees, and is the main reason to prefer landless workers. The preference of managers of Vapi factories for migrant workers rests on the same principle. Their argument to employ migrant labour is precisely the same as the reason why employers say they prefer local landless workers. A manager of a large garment factory at Vapi, employing several thousands of workers, of which 50 per cent are migrants from Bihar and UP, reasons that 'local labour does not bother, they own land and crops, and work for their own requirements to go to movies and not for their families. People from Uttar Pradesh and Biharis do the heavy work, they have to provide for the living of their families there.'

The present head of village (*sarpanch*) of Lalgam is a Dhodia from Piruwadi. Dhodias, who have four out of seven seats on the village council, are numerically dominant. Six of these seven seats have been reserved for Scheduled Castes and Scheduled Tribes. The Dhodia majority signifies their numerical importance and local social prominence compared to other Scheduled Tribes. An Anavil occupies the unreserved seat.

Compared to the villages in the 1970s, the major part of Piruwadi where Dhodias reside looks more prosperous. The outer appearance and interiors of their houses are important indications. The majority of the houses still have the characteristic broad 'Dhodia shape', with a high veranda that forms the covered front of the house used for sitting (and sleeping when it is hot). The roofs of these houses are slanted, with their edges extending beyond the walls, which are a couple of feet above the ground. These houses are still made of wooden beams, mud, and cow dung. The thatched roofs that covered these houses in the 1970s, however, almost all have tiled roofs now.

These houses generally accommodate husband, wife, and children, the husband's aged parents, and his unmarried siblings. Their interiors certainly differ from those 30 years ago. There are TV sets and a small compact audio system. The furniture also includes several iron cupboards to store clothes and other valuables; a plastic covered sofa; a few folding chairs; and woodframe double beds covered with foam mattresses instead of *katla* (string cots).

Often a ceiling fan hangs on the wooden beam which supports the low roof, threatening to behead tall and inattentive visitors.

Kitchens look different too: they are furnished with some stainless steel kitchenware stored in wood frames. Women use kerosene stoves, electrical cooking rings, or even twin-burner gas stoves and gas cylinders, though they never do without *chuhlas* (the traditional fireplace). Sometimes there is a fridge, which serves the neighbours too.

Houses are decorated with pictures of deities and there is always a shrine dedicated the one of the gods such as Hanuman and Shankar. In almost every house one finds pictures of gurus like Swaminarayan, Maharaj and Asaram Bapu. The latter is a living saint, one out of many in India who became popular among Dhodias in the last 10 to 15 years.

Of course, this is not true for all Dhodia houses. There are dwellings whose inhabitants are too poor to afford luxuries, and some houses look more prosperous than others. There are also some recently built brick houses with one or two storeys.

In Piruwadi the great majority of Dhodias resides in different *faliyas*.

One of the most remarkable features of these Dhodia *faliyas* is that in almost each *faliya* there are one or two *pacca*[1] houses made of brick among a conglomerate of *kaccha* dwellings. These structures show the differential social and economic upward mobility that has occurred among Dhodias over the past several decades (Punalekar, 1980: 50ff). Much of the detailed information and examples that follow will illuminate how 30 years of industrialization has contributed to this process.

It is important to point out that this differential upward mobility occurs within and between groups of people residing in Piruwadi and the village of Lalgam. Social and economic progress diverges among Dhodias, but even more so between Dhodias and others like Naikas or Dublas.

WORSHIP

Hanuman *faliya* is one of the Dhodia *faliyas* in Piruwadi. It consists of a maze of nine *kaccha* houses and sheds and a recently built two-storey brick house. These 10 structures, housing a total of more than 50 inhabitants, accommodates 10 married cousins and their families. These men have a common great grandfather who came to Piruwadi around 1900 to become a tenant of a Bania moneylender.

The faliya owes its name to the monkey god Hanuman, and one of the cousins has made a shrine in his honour in one of his sheds.

In this case Hanuman is huge pear-shaped stone. It has been painted red and at the top, which could be considered the head, there are two white eyes with black pupils. Numerous crumpled printed images of different deities, welted flowers, and a small statue of Hanuman cover the front of the stone. The Dhodia, a senior clerk in a local high school, told the following story about the origin of the stone and Hanuman:

For many years on his way to his work, from the bridge he had seen the stone lying in the Auranga River. One day, when, as usual, he crossed the bridge on his motorbike, he slipped and crashed. The only damage done was a torn shirt. While he lay on the bridge he could see the stone. He was sure that Hanuman had saved him. He felt attracted to him since his childhood because Hanuman is very strong, does not die, and had always helped him.[2]

After the incident he consulted a known *bhagat*[3] from another village who told him that 'Hanumanji was willing to come to his house'. So he decided to bring the stone to his *faliya*. First he tried to do it by hand, with the help of many people. After this unsuccessful attempt he decided to rent a crane, chains, and helpers to hoist the stone out of the riverbed. A Tempo (three-wheeler) carried the stone to the *faliya* in Piruwadi. Villagers and the *bhagat* still regularly worship the stone.

Two of the ten cousins living in the Hanuman *faliya* are ex-employees of the chemical plant Atul-Atic. They were pensioned off a few years ago. One owns the brick house, which he built with money received after his early retirement.

The other ex-employee of Atul-Atic intends to begin constructing a brick house when the monsoon is over. The father of the present absentee-landlord of Piruwadi employed the ex-employee's father as *mukadam*. He had to recruit and supervise workers to cut the grass that covered the lands of the Anavil.

The Dhodia lives with his three married sons who are between 30 and 35 years old. One 'sits at home' and is unemployed. The second son is a 'mechanic' and works in a nearby service station on the road to Gundlav Estate. The third son drives his own rickshaw. He used to be a 'fitter', pulling toe strips through a hole in the soles of the slippers made in a slipper factory in Gundlav. He was a contract worker earning about Rs. 38 per day. His wife used to work in a Chain establishment for Rs. 25 per day. The family is one of the five families from Hanuman *faliya* that still own a few *bighas* of cultivable land on which they grow paddy. To harvest the crop, they call on Dublas who live just across the highway. The yield feeds the family for 3 to 4 months. The family became owners of the land as a result of the Tenancy Acts, which state that land should belong to the tiller. That's why the 75-year-old grandfather of the family holds the late Indira Gandhi in great respect. He says that it was during her term of office that the land became his property. The system of divisible inheritance, however, left the other five families with parcels of land too tiny to be cultivated.

Each time I visited the *faliya*, which I used to do in the evening around 7 o'clock, I heard people singing *bhajans* (religious songs) accompanied by a harmonium and finger cymbals. The gatherings took place in the brick house adjoining the *kaccha* houses. Unlike the inhabitants of other Dhodia *faliyas* located closer to the periphery of Piruwadi, the occupants of the Hanuman *faliya* are known to be decent people and said to abstain from alcohol. They are followers of Asaram Bapu. Older men from the *faliya* articulated the importance of their guru. 'He is like a God, he descends from the ancient Hindu past. He shows us how to live. He knows the right way . . . he gives happiness. . . . He has books with exercises to cease drinking and smoking.'

Asaram Bapu provides happiness for many Dhodias. Among this group is a divorced woman. After her husband left her to live with another woman, she and her son returned to her father's house in Piruwadi. Her reputation suffered, and she is considered a menace to men in the village and in the factory where she works. Another example is the man who managed to stop drinking because it had almost ruined his body and family. He explained how Asaram Bapu had helped him abstain from alcohol.

INTERMEZZO: THE CONTENT AND MEANING OF ASARAM'S TEACHINGS

Asaram Bapu is popular in Gujarat. His headquarters are in Ahmedabad, and he runs the main *ashram* in Surat. His teachings, inspired by the Vedas and Upanishads, attract thousands of listeners and devotees. They listen to him in large assembly halls (*mandap*) where he appears live or on video screens. These halls and *ashrams* are found all over Gujarat: in Rajkot, Palanpur, and Vadodara. A few years ago he opened a large *mandap* on the outskirts of Vapi Industrial Estate. He also has many followers and *ashrams* in neighboring states and abroad—in Singapore, Kenya, the USA, and the UK. His treatises and teachings are available, in English as well as Hindi, as printed texts and video cassettes and can be purchased from stalls at his *ashrams* and halls. Below follows the essence of two lectures that provide good examples of the content of his message. To preserve their tone and tenor, the quotations are from the English translations. The first text is called 'The Vedantic message of fearlessness' (Asaramji Maharaj 1995a). It teaches that:

> When people detach themselves from worldly affairs they do not have to be afraid. Then there is no reason to be depressed or dejected when outward happenings are unfavourable. Because all power, glory and self-confidence spring from fearlessness, people must be peaceful and brave. Misfortune even may be for someone's own good in the end. Misery will follow as long as people identify with flesh, bones and lust. The greatest misery is the cycle of birth and death.
>
> Those who are impressed by others or movies are unaware of their own majesty. Nobody is greater than, and nothing goes beyond that situation or condition. People should experience that they are God. Be sure to be Brahman and 'experience your omnipotent nature and you become omnipotent'. Wealth, power and prestige are illusions. Why do you consider yourself to be lowly, weak, downtrodden, and a sinner? Through Vedanta learn that the entire universe is your creation . . . (W)hy don't you take yourself to be the fearless, independent incarnation of God? (ibid.: 24, 26).
>
> In another treatise, 'Glory of eternal youth', Asaram addresses the youth (Asaramji Maharaj 1995b). The preface, written by somebody else, criticizes contemporary Indian society as too materialistic and sensual. This condition deprives youth from the country's rich and beautiful cultural heritage. Artificial lifestyles rob society of its lustre and thereby make life miserable. It leads to bad habits among young like masturbation, unnatural sex, addiction to intoxicants and diseases.
>
> Asaram starts his lecture by observing that the body is a tool to perform religious rites and that when it is weak it will influence the mind. This weakness is caused by the gratification of physical desires which saps away the energy and vitality of the body. Today's society stimulates the loss of vital energy because of pornographic literature. It leads to bad habits displayed in movies and on television, and waste of seminal energy through masturbation. One way to prevent this and protect the semen is to keep the mode of living simple. The idea that a life of pomp and extravagance confers status in society is false. The more ostentatious one's life is, the more difficult it becomes to protect the semen.
>
> The other way to prevent the loss of seminal energy is to stay away from intoxicants because alcohol, cigarettes, and tobacco excite sexual lust and passion. The third way to control lust is to see all women as mother and to see others' wealth as a pile of dust.

Conditions of social and cultural subordination in the village of Lalgam and in the other villages of south Gujarat *asaram's* explain *asaram's* popularity among Dhodias. In place of abasing stereotypes and value judgements like 'backward', without 'morals' and 'drunkards', people are approached as dignified human beings who do not need to 'feel low and downtrodden', and addressed as 'incarnations of God and Brahman'.

His quotations from Hindu religious texts are important as well. Asaram talks to his audiences as Hindus and urges his listeners to share ideas and ways of life that go with upper-class Hinduism. By preaching a sober and detached life without 'intoxicants' and 'lust satisfaction', he offers a means to lead a decent life, a way out of misery and towards salvation. His critique of today's materialism and lifestyles, and the illusionary nature of wealth and status may provide comfort by reconciling people who have not experienced improvements in their material and social conditions. Rising incomes, more purchasing power, and increased consumption are primarily urban phenomena.

PIRUWADI AGAIN

Another recently built brick Dhodia house is located in the centre of Piruwadi, at the end of its blacktop road next to the primary school. In the front yard there is a motorbike, a small Maruti van, and a Tempo three-wheeler. Unlike other brick Dhodia houses, it stands alone and is not part of a *faliya*. This stand-alone house was the result of the owner and his family moving away from the lands of his father, which were part of the present Anavil absentee landlord's in Piruwadi. The family lived on the lands of the Anavil whom the father served as a landless labourer. In the 1950s the Anavil, who was the village head, decided to move the Dhodias and settle them on government property, where they still reside.

The owner of the house is an employee of Atul-Atic and still remembers the poverty when he was young. That's why he is angry with his grandchildren when they do not want to eat: '(T)here is so much food now . . . I was used to having only one meal a day. Sometimes I could eat because my mother did not take food.' He began his career in Atul-Atic as a contract worker in the gang of a Dhodia *mukadam* whom he knew. At that time he was one of the few people in Piruwadi with a job in Atul-Atic. Later he was employed permanently as a 'helper'. Now he drives a forklift in one of the retail departments of the company, earning Rs. 6,500 per month, or about Rs. 250 per day. He admitted he has been lucky. He financed the construction of his house through advances from his provident fund and from loans obtained from the Atul-Atic credit society. His wage receipts show monthly deductions to repay debts. Private loans helped him buy his motorbike, car, and his son's three-wheeler.

A job at Atul-Atic provided financial means and credibility to improve status because it became possible to build a house and show improved prosperity and status.

The Dhodia told that men derive *ijjat* from factory labour because 'there are all sorts of facilities'. It is much better than to work on the land of somebody else. 'The best is to be a farmer with your own land.' He believes that 'for women factory labour is bad because there are too many men around. But sometimes women have to work in factories because money is needed'.

His three sons stay in the same house, two of them are married. The unmarried youngest son sits in a small shop next to the house. He sells soft drinks, bidis, cigarettes and sweets. The second son drives the Tempo three-wheeler to transport goods on the nearby industrial estate of Gundlav.

The third son calls himself a mechanic. He is temporarily employed for more than six years in a small engineering factory at Gundlav, earning Rs. 60 per day.

CAUSES OF DIFFERENTIATION

These examples do not suggest that 30 years of industrialization were the sole cause of upward mobility among the Dhodias. For instance, another Dhodia, owner of a recently built two-storey *pacca* house, has been employed permanently by the Gujarat State Transport Company for many years. At present he earns Rs. 7,000 per month, or almost Rs. 270 per day.

Upward mobility among the Dhodias is the result of a combination of favourable conditions: industrial employment is only one of these. Traditionally Dhodias have been better situated, both economically and socially, than other tribal groups such as the Kukna, Naika, or Dubla. The most important factor to economic and social progress has been the political importance of the Dhodias, which is a result of their numerical prominence, adult suffrage, and the constituency voting system. These led to better implementation of tenancy laws and measures of 'protective discrimination' aimed at raising Scheduled Castes and Scheduled Tribes. These conditions contributed to the changed quality of their economic, social, and religious life in the first place.

The type of industrial employment during the last 30 years does, however, account for differences between families. Permanent employees of Atul-Atic are paid more, enjoy better secondary facilities, and obtain loans easier than the majority of workers employed by smaller factories in the region. It enabled these villagers to broaden the economic base of their households and to improve their social status. They did this, in part, by disapproving of factory labour for women, certainly married women, and by building *pacca* houses. By pursuing a more pious Hindu style of life, Dhodias felt they could attain greater religious prestige, which was very important.

Dhodias employed permanently in smaller factories in the region show similar traits, albeit to a lesser extent. One such worker is a 45-year-old operator in a chemical factory, earning a monthly salary of Rs. 4,000, which is about Rs. 153 per day. The factory, which employs about 200 workers, is located not far from Piruwadi along one of the roads leading out of Bulsar.

Opposite his small parental house, located in a *faliya* closer to the periphery of Piruwadi, he and his two other brothers had built in the 1980s a row of *kaccha* dwellings sharing one veranda and one roof. The different rooms accommodate the separate households of the three married brothers plus their parents. His fourth brother, who is much younger and still unmarried, also occupies a room in the house. Two of his brothers are permanent workers employed by factories at Gundlav Estate. The youngest brother is a contract labourer working in a drug manufacturing plant.

The operator, the eldest of the four brothers, still remembers the poverty when he was young; his father owned only 2 acres of cultivable land. They are more prosperous now 'because all brothers are employed in *ji ai di si* (GIDC)'.[4] He does not allow his daughters to work in factories, certainly not in Chain Electricals because 'employment there has little *ijjat*'. Without any prompting, he asserts that he is a religious man and a follower of *Moksh Marg*.[5] He shows a large framed picture with portraits of many gods and holy men. He knows them all and calls them 'Brahma, Vishnu, Shankar, Suresh, and Swaminarayan'. He explains that

> 'one should follow dharma, the way to God. You can better be a poor man with dharma, than be rich without it.' For his daily life it means that he performs puja each morning for one hour, that he does not drink or smoke, and does not eat in 'hotels' because he is vegetarian. 'One has to be a good person.' Being a good person now does not mean for him that he will be a Brahmin, Desai or Bania in his next life. 'No, I am not sure, because nowadays these people all are non-vegetarian. I want to be a vegetarian in my next life.'

Life has been different for Dhodia workers who have been continuously employed as temperwali in one of the many hazardous smaller factories.

One of them began his career in a small, newly opened chemical plant at Gundlav in 1969. Between then and now his working life has been interrupted by accidents. For instance, in 1977 when he was still a temperwali, an explosion in the Gundlav factory released chloric gases which killed three people. The factory was closed and the Dhodia found a job in a chemical factory in Mumbai. In that factory he met with a serious accident disfiguring his right arm. He had to leave the job without any financial compensation and returned to Piruwadi. He worked for a few years in a chemical factory at Gundlav but had to stop because his disfigured arm and bad health did not allow for heavy work any longer. At present he earns a little by casual labour and by doing odd jobs in the village.

The above description shows the link between differential upward mobility among Dhodias of Piruwadi and the type of industrial employment they had. This link raises speculation about the prospects of the second generation of industrial workers. More precisely, will the sons[6] of more prosperous workers be able to consolidate the economic and social achievements of their fathers? And, second, will the sons of less fortunate Dhodias be able to catch up? Although it is difficult to predict, the growing casualization of industrial work makes for a certain degree of pessimism. The increasing preference of owners and managers to use workers employed by labour contractors means that it will be even more unlikely for industrial workers to move from unskilled temperwalis to experienced permanent workers.

For an increasing number of villagers the 'Atul-route',[7] which had represented a chance at attaining greater income, security, and prestige, will be closed. Revealing is the despair voiced by younger Dhodia workers like Nanu, the younger brother of the *Moksh Marg* disciple quoted earlier.

Nanu is 27 years old and unmarried. His face, arms, and hands are covered with large black and white spots. He owes them to acid spilled in the chemical factory of his former employer. He had been employed in this factory as a casual worker for several years, earning Rs. 31 per day. At present he is a contract worker in a drug manufacturing company located along the nearby NH 8. He earns the minimum wage of Rs. 61 per day without any benefits. He lives in a room in the long *kaccha* house where his three married brothers and their wives maintain three separate households. He boards with one of them, paying his *bhabhi* (wife of his older brother) Rs. 400 per month. 'There is no chance of being employed permanently, you are removed when you raise the subject. . . . There is too much bossing. If the manager tells [you] to sit down, you have to sit, if he wants you to get up, you must stand up. When you object you are fired . . . I want more money, a normal life, a wife and children. Now I am too poor to marry.'

He shares some agricultural land with his three brothers which provides the 25 family members with rice for a period of three months. My question about why he does not buy a pump to increase his agricultural income he answers with: 'How can you say this . . . one can hardly survive on Rs. 1,600. You need Rs. 40,000 to buy a pump set and money for drilling. I tried to get a loan under some scheme. First I had to bribe everybody in the office and finally the manager told me that I did not get a loan because I could not pay it back. . . .' He continues our conversation by telling that 'now it is more difficult than it had been for workers because there is much more contract work now and more people want jobs because the population has increased. I am unhappy and worried, I am afraid I will have an accident again. I cannot pay the hospital and I would rather be dead.'

Other young men display the same feelings. In the afternoon after Diwali, along one of the small paths connecting two *faliyas* in Piruwadi, five young men sit together and enjoy their holiday by chatting and drinking.

When I join them they explain that 'this is how we relax, we don't drink daily, but once a week or so'. They are all contract workers. Without any prompting, they start complaining about the government and contractors. 'Inspectors are not interested in us' and 'labour contractors don't show any respect.' The contract of one of the men has been terminated some time ago. Despite vacancies in the factory where he used to work, he sits at home. The contractor did not call him: 'To get a job through contractors one needs influence. If you want work in Atul-Atic you have to pay the contractor.' And, again, 'when you complain or join a union, you are fired immediately. We feel *lachari* (helpless).'

The conditions and mood of these young workers and those of older Dhodia temperwalis correspond more with the experiences of other industrial workers in the village of Lalgam than with those of their more prosperous *jatibhaio*. Their experience with 30 years of industrial development is not the same as that of the Dhodia industrial workers of Lalgam. It certainly is not representative of what other tribals like Naikas and Dublas residing in Lalgam and living in other south Gujarati villages experienced during the past three decades of industrialization.

Then and now Dhodias have been better situated than Kuknas, Naikas, and Dublas with regard to subsistence and prestige, social access, and political leverage. Dhodias were able to participate in the industrial development of south Gujarat from its earliest stage onwards. Though, initially, in the 1960s and 1970s, they had been employed mostly as unskilled workers on a temporary basis, the fortunate among them in Piruwadi and other villages were able to take the 'Atul route' to social mobility. For the Naikas and Dublas of Lalgam, and those living elsewhere in south Gujarat, this opportunity hardly arose and still does not exist. To earn a living they have no option other than to offer their unskilled, cheap labour to perform temporary physical work in workshops and small, hazardous, poorly equipped factories or seek employment as casual workers in large factories. Their conditions do not differ much from those of the early 1970s. The final paragraphs of this chapter illustrate this: they present the tale of some Naikas interviewed in the 1970s and again in 1998.

PAST AND PRESENT OF A WORKERS' FAMILY

In 1974 I interviewed members of an Adivasi family who were among workers I regularly met. They resided in makeshift dwellings at the periphery of the village of Lalgam, along one of the roads leading out of Bulsar near the present NH 8.

In 1974 they were all temporarily employed in small neighbouring factories such as Happy Chemicals, which produced dyes and chemicals; one of the first Chain establishments producing plastic switches; or firms which produced wooden textile bobbins. They earned not more than Rs. 3 per day, the standard remuneration for unskilled and temporary labour at that time. The eldest among those present, who used to be a landless labourer serving Anavils, was the first to explain the important difference between landowning and landless industrial workers. Chagan, his son, supported him by telling about the plans to undertake an action in Happy Chemicals meant to improve working conditions and increase wages.

I met the family again in 1998. The father who told about the animosities between landowning and landless workers died long ago. Two cousins succumbed to TB some years later. A third cousin, Bana, still works in a Chain establishment. Chagan and his younger brother Sunil are unemployed.

Chagan, Sunil and Bana are still neighbours, their *kachha* houses are small and empty. *Khatla* occupy most of the space inside. Kitchens lack kitchenware and stock, there are fireplaces with some twigs, a little firewood, and a few earthen jars filled with water.

Chagan and Sunil had been temperwali in Happy Chemicals between 1970 and 1993. In 1974 they had been called to the house of one of the Desais to do all kinds of odd jobs, like cutting grass or washing dishes during the lavish wedding feast of his daughter.

The concern has been one of the first in a series of small chemical factories in Bulsar run by Anavil Brahmins (Desais). They manufactured all sorts of chemicals to be used by Atul-Atic, where other Desais hold executive positions. I described the rise of Anavil industrial entrepreneurs in Bulsar in the late 1960s as '(w)hen one lamp starts moving, others will follow' (Streefkerk, 1985: 151 ff.). Happy Chemicals consisted of a collection of small sheds and firms with their own names: Mr. Blue and Sons, Laxmi Dyes and Saraswati Intermediates. In 1993 it was closed because one Desai stopped working and the other expired. He financed the building of the Desai Cricket Stadium and Sports Complex of Bulsar, which accommodates a swimming pool.

In 1998 Sunil told about his loyalty to Happy Chemicals. After he had heard that the owners might suffer from financial problems he collected money to enable the Desais to pay their bills. Earlier, the Desais lent him money for his daughter's marriage and paid for his medical expenses.

He is unemployed since Happy Chemicals was closed. He and his wife depend on the earnings of their son. He is a peon in the office at a nearby factory, where 'he brings water and moves papers', earning Rs. 50 per day. It is not much but the work gives more *ijjat* (prestige) than factory labour, according to the father.

During the last 24 years Chagan had changed from a tall handsome youth into a weak, worn-out old man. His face was pockmarked, an egg-shaped swelling jutted from his neck, both hands were covered with numerous small black holes, and the skin of his legs was ruined. 'All due to the chemicals with which I worked for 30 years' while mentioning pains he pointed to his back, hips, and stomach.

The closure of Happy Chemicals in 1993 was the biggest misfortune of his life. He lost his regular income of Rs. 35 per day. To feed his wife, two daughters, and a small mentally handicapped son, he depends on casual labour. At present the family needs Rs. 850 per month to survive. Sometimes he earns more and is able to save for the next month, but this is not often the case. Ordinarily the family has to make do with the irregular amounts his wife and unmarried daughters earn through casual work in neighbouring factories, supplemented by money borrowed from neighbours, friends, and shopkeepers. When we talked about his life, misfortunes and happiness, he referred to dignity. He proudly mentioned that he did not eat meat, smoke, or drink.

Not all villagers were abstainers. Elsewhere in the village I discovered—because men rushed out of her hut while I entered it in the afternoon—an aged woman who distilled liquor illicitly. In this part of the village, inhabited by poor landless workers, male inhabitants became drunk between 6 and 8 o'clock in the evening.

The work of David Hardiman on the Devi movement (1984) and on the politics of drinking among the Adivasis in colonial south

Gujarat (1985) clarifies the origin of the use of alcohol and Chagan's ideals. Long ago, country liquor (*daru*), made from the flower of the *mahua* tree, and toddy[8] were cheap and important nutritional elements of Advisasi diet because it contained calories and vitamins. Toddy helped them to digest the coarse and heavy unleavened breads and was of great importance during hot season when other food was hardly available. *Daru* and toddy were considered to be beneficial against malaria, cholera and plague (Hardiman, 1985: 176). They also had an important religious and social meaning.

In 1878 colonial authorities imposed controls over the production and sale of liquor for moral and financial reasons. Only official approved distilleries could produce alcohol. Authorities deprived Adivasis of unadulterated and cheap alcohol,[9] criminalized them, and drove them into the clutches of Parsi liquor dealers in their villages. The latter was one of the reasons for the rise the Devi[10] movement among Adivasis in south Gujarat between 1922 and 1923. The movement represented an act of assertion against the most rapacious of the local exploiters, the Parsis (Hardiman, 1985: 212). It can also be seen as a dramatic example of the process of tribal Sanskritization because the movement preached new rules of purity by abstaining from meat and drink (Hardiman, 1984: 213).[11] Hardiman also observes that later on prominent members forged an alliance with middle-class Gandhi nationalists of Gujarat who opposed drinking too (Hardiman, 1985: 214).

Chagan's dignity, and that of many of his companions, seems to emanate from the lifestyle of high-caste Hindus. This conformity is a sign of Sanskritization and confirms the hegemony of the regional culture of Brahmins and Banias, who are still among the most powerful in south Gujarat (Hardiman, 1984: 218). It is, perhaps, hard to admit that Chagan's standards, and those of others, are preferences of people who are superiors in many respects.

CONCLUSION

Growing economic and social differentiation characterizes the industrial labour force. As was the case 30 years ago, the worker-peasants are predominantly Dhodias, Naikas, and Dublas who do not intermarry and have a hierarchical relationship. They remain the least privileged groups in the society. Because of their initial social, economic, and political lead, the Dhodias have been more successful over the last four decades.

Local industrial employment mirrors these inequalities. From the beginning, Dublas and Naikas have been employed as temporary workers in small workshops and larger factories to perform unskilled tasks under unsafe conditions with primitive tools and dangerous machinery. Thirty years of industrial employment has brought these workers hardly any economic improvement and has often left them with ruined bodies. Industrialization has perpetuated the earlier social and economic conditions through the next generation. Sons and daughters have to start their lives from the same poor and inferior positions as their parents did.

For Dhodias recent history has been different. Although not all were successful, some have become more prosperous; they have raised their social status by discouraging their women from working in factories and enhanced their religious prestige. The type of industrial employment they have engaged in has been one of the reasons why some have been able to prosper and others not. Those employed by the chemical complex of Atul-Atic and smaller factories as permanent workers with higher wages and benefits have been able to attain greater security, material welfare, and prestige than Dhodias employed as temperwalis in one of the many smaller factories or workshops. Greater casualization, however, makes the continuation of upward mobility into the next generation of industrial workers unlikely. Instead, feelings of deprivation will grow because the younger generation of workers enjoys less prosperity and security than its fathers or older members of the families and *jati*. This generation's exposure to middle class lifestyles in the neighbouring town and to TV commercials continuously emphasizing the glamour of consumer goods, ranging from toothpaste to private cars, certainly contribute to these feelings.

Religious fervour among many industrial workers who are Dhodias is another important feature of local industrial transformation. It is not at all unusual for members of a mobile subaltern group to adopt the religious practices and ways of life of the dominant Hindu population in order to raise their status. This explanation, known as Sanskritization, is in accord with observations made by Punelaker in his study of the Dhodias of Surat city (1980: 32, 33). He writes that upper strata among the Dhodias worship Hindu gods, and that they (especially the educated and landowning Dhodias) have been influenced by sects like Moksh Marg and Swaminarayan[12] during the past decades. Dedication to Asaram Bapu can be seen as a local manifestation of this trend. This guru is not very popular among the Dublas, the poorest inhabitants of the village of Lalgam. They comment that they lack time and money to dedicate themselves to 'one of these bapus', and they 'cannot afford to visit them'. They confirm the theory that economic betterment precedes Sanskritization.

Devotion can also be interpreted as a contemporary way of emulating the lifestyles of members of the local urban middle class. Dedication to a 'variety of gurus and godmen' is part of urban middle class culture, according to Panini (1996: 54). These gurus include Sai Baba of Puttaparuti, Chinmayananda, Muktanada, Dadji, Nirmala Devi, and others 'who attract hordes of devotees from the middle class'. He characterizes the lifestyle of members of the new middle classes as materialist, aimed at the acquisition and display of a wide range of consumer goods (Panini: 53). I do not know the social composition of the guru's followers. In the region of Bulsar it is said that his followers are mainly of 'lower class' origins. Yet, there are strong indications that he also has numerous adherents among middle class inhabitants of Bulsar and among members of the middle classes in cities like Surat, Vadodara, and Ahmedabad.

It is possible that BJP and related organizations, whose members and leaders advocate Hindu nationalism, support the guru. Hinduization of the tribals of south Gujarat, who constitute the majority of its population, would further broaden BJP's political base (Joshi 1999).[13]

The most likely explanation of Asaram's popularity would probably combine several of the above explanations, with the addition ofone that more explicitly emphasizes the meaning of Asaram and his teachings for his followers. Such an interpretation must stress different meanings for different groups of people.

Asaram Bapu can help members of the urban middle class to overcome their feelings of moral degeneration arising from their addiction to new wealth and consumption. Wessel (1998) recently discovered this emotional predicament among members of the

Vadodara middle class. By attending his meetings, buying video cassettes, watching him and listening to lessons about the illusionary nature of wealth, they can salve their consciences. In any case, his anti-materialism and anti-modernism comfort numerous members of the urban middle classes who are less well-to-do and cannot conform to new standards of consumption and display.

For the much less prosperous Dhodias of Piruwadi the importance of the guru and his messages centre on their past and present social and cultural subordination and deprivation. Rather than abasing value judgements, they are approached as dignified human beings and Hindus who should not feel inferior. His emphasis on personal merit, on the insignificance of wealth and status, and his disapproval of materialism, consoles those who still are, or feel deprived. At the same time, devotion and the appeal to the guru's imputed spiritual powers help people to cope with uncertainties and to face personal hardship and suffering.

NOTES

1. *Pacca* means pure, ritually clean as opposed to *kaccha*. Both meanings relate to food in particular. When used metaphorically *pacca* denotes solid, strong and prestigious, *kaccha* means the opposite.
2. Most villages in south Gujarat have a shrine dedicated to Hanuman. Roy and Rizvi (1985: 101, 102) write that the local population asserts that they have been worshipping Hanuman for ages. He is said to protect their villages and keep away all diseases.
3. The *bhagat* is the priest-cum-faith healer of the Dhodia population of a village. He used to read out the Hanuman texts during ceremonies dedicated to him (Hardiman, 2002: 101, 108).
4. In the local language the abbreviation GIDC stands for factories in the industrial estate of Gundlav. GIDC means 'Gujarat Industrial Development Corporation'. It is the state organization which is responsible for the development of industrial estates at Gundlav, Vapi and elsewhere in Gujarat.
5. Pillai (1976: 47) writes how in Dharampur State, *Moksha Marg*, a religious reformist movement preaching to give up liquor, extended its infuence among Adivasi families in the early decades of the former century. During the second half of last century, *Moksha Marg* became widespread among Adivasis and others in the whole of south Gujarat. *Moksha Marg* means *path to* (Hindu) *salvation*. Hindu salvation is the liberation from the eternal cycle of birth, death, and rebirth.

6. One can also read much younger brothers or cousins of first generation workers, instead of sons.
7. The Atul-route is meant metaphorically, the term also includes factories smaller than Atul-Atic and offering permanent jobs, higher wages and benefits as well.
8. Toddy is the fermented juice of any kind of palm tree.
9. Toddy trees were taxed and toddy tapping required a (British) government license.
10. The name Devi movement has its origin in the Devi (goddess) of Salahbai, generally represented by an image, and believed to originate in the mountains in the east.
11. The Hindu sect Swaminarayan also forbids the use of animal food, drinks and drugs.
12. The powerful and popular Hindu sect Swaminarayan, started as a reform-movement in Gujarat round 1820. It became a global movement due to Gujarati migration to East-Africa, and later-on, to England and the USA. It owes its present powerful position in Gujarat to Gujarati immigrants in the UK and USA (Rutten, 2003: 11).
13. In the village like in Gujarat as a whole, political support changed from Congress to BJP.

CHAPTER 7

POSTSCRIPT

The search ends where it began. I looked for a way to understand what I saw in south Gujarat by beginning with the seminal thinkers of the nineteenth century and their followers in the 1950s and 1960s. Ultimately I returned to Marx, Weber, and their contemporaries and how they understood what happened around them in Europe between 1800 and 1900. When their writings are stripped of ethnocentrism and Orientalism, their discourses still address relevant questions. They call attention to crucial features of capitalist industrialization that may be compelling and universal: production in specialized organizations equipped with machines powered by non-animate sources of energy; workers who do not own industrial instruments of production, who only have their labour power to sell; and physical separation between household and workplace. These features are causes and consequences of industrial capitalism and are revolutionary as tendencies. Capitalist industrialization can break down existing loyalty relationships, such as kinship, local, regional, and ethnic attachments. Impersonal market and administration procedures favour rationalization and secularization. Questions of cohesion, identity and loyalties, alienation and rationalization occupied Marx, Weber, and other important nineteenth-century thinkers; these topics are still pertinent. Issues of social identity, loyalties, integration, and related questions of estrangement or alienation and disenchantment are all issues of capitalist modernity.

The history of Gujarat since the past 300 years reveals long- and short-term continuities in the transition from pre-manufacturing industry to industrial capitalist enterprise (Streefkerk, 1997).[1] The role of entrepreneurship in this transformation has been 'not-so-mysterious' or 'non-problematical' at all. The Brahmin Ranchodlal illustrates this idea. He established the first textile mill in Ahmedabad in 1861.[2] A London-based Indian businessman procured British machines and shipped them to India. The absence of railways forced Ranchodlal to transport the parts by bullock carts from the harbour of

Cambay to the city of Ahmedabad, where an English expert installed the machines (Mehta, 1982: 35-53). Indian entrepreneurs owned 25 textile mills in the city in 1898, they had 53 mills in 1916 (Mehta: 156-65). Actually, industrial enterpreneurship shows a striking continuity overtime (Streefkerk, 1997). Those situated strategically in terms of influence, finance, or skills, have been able to combine nature, labour and capital in an efficient manner. They have certainly been able to do so during the last four decades of industrial transition.

The initial stage of local industrialization in south Gujarat evinces the importance of existing social configurations in establishing capitalist industrialization. Craftsmanship and economic and political promi-nence determined future industrial enterpreneurship. Relations of vicinity and inequality enabled personal and efficient control of labour. The mobilization of capital, knowledge, and organization of sales occurred, as they did in Europe, through primordial relations. In south Gujarat these relations were based on kinship, friendship, and caste.

Another continuity is the persistence in the subordinate manner through which labour has been employed in pre-machine industry and capitalist enterprise. Recent research shows the extremely poor and inferior conditions of workers in south Gujarat then (Streefkerk, 1997) and now (Breman, 1985b). The appalling, unprotected, living and working conditions of labour at the industrial estate of Vapi are the most recent manifestations of the restrained nature of capitalist exploitation between Tapi and Vapi.

One manifestation of capitalist modernity in Bulsar is the combination of industrialization and caste. Suthars, and others, show that after six decades of industrialization the 'spirit' of caste is still alive.[3] They also demonstrate that recognizing 'caste on the ground' is easier than finding its definition (Fuller, 1996: 25). The definition should include the principle of purity-impurity. It partly explains caste's hierarchy (Kolenda, 1984: 62; Srinivas 1996: ix). It should also contain the importance of caste endogamy. Endogamy maintains caste purity (Dube, 1996: 16). During the last century the purity-impurity distinction became less rigid in both the public and occupational domains and caste inequalities cannot be legitimately endorsed in public since Independence (Fuller, 1996: 21). The purity-impurity principle, however, still dominates matrimony and the domestic sphere: 'The kitchen may be described as the heart of the purity-impurity system' (Srinivas, 1996: ix).

Caste retained its spirit but its form and function changed during the last century. *Enlargement of scale*, a feature of capitalist industrialization, touched caste as well. The emergence of huge caste groups, or *horizontal stretch* (Srinivas, 1979: 241), is the contemporary expression of caste. Caste associations are a concrete manifestation of this tendency. Some associations and federations were organized to secure political position, as was the case with the Kshatriya Sabha of Central Gujarat (Shah, 1975). Others came into existence for mainly social and educational reasons (Engelshoven, 1993: 137-42). In south Gujarat caste stretched as well. In the middle regions of local social configuration it served as a major frame of identity and loyalty.

Rutten (2003: 11) describes how Patidars from Kaira district in the USA and in the UK emphasized old loyalties during the 1970s and 1980s. In these countries they initiated organizations based on caste, subcaste, marriage circles, and village of origin. They brought back primordial loyalties to their villages in Gujarat, where they awoke sleeping caste-organizations of Patidars. This exemple shows the international stretch of caste and its contribution to Anderson's *long-distance nationalism* (1992).

In Bulsar, capitalist industrialization led to the rise of a middle class and signs of a shared consciousness. The trends among middle class Suthars presented in Chapter 5, however, indicate a different tendency. They articulate caste consciousness. The Panchal Sewa Samaj, the Suthar caste association revived in the 1980s, expresses this trend. Caste remains, for rich and poor, a major frame of loyalty and identity. My hypothesis is that caste consciousness accompanies the rise of the urban middle class. Caste consciousness is found among groups that constitute this class-in-itself.

At the lower end of the local social scale, among the industrial workers, caste or community also kept its significance. For Dhodias, who constitute a considerable proportion of all industrial workers in south Gujarat, their caste continued to be an important frame reference. They remained organized in kin groups, living in adjacent dwellings, in lineages of three to four generations, while endogamy retained its pre-eminence. They distinguished themselves from others, whom they considered to be 'high', or 'low' people.

Dhodias and other industrial workers like Naikas exhibit signs of

Sanskritization and their religious fervour is a salient feature. Many Dhodias and other worker-peasants are followers of Asaram Bapu, a living saint.

A second manifestation of capitalist modernity during the first decades of industrialization is the continued importance of religion. The erection of the huge *mandap* and *ashram* of Asaram Bapu at Vapi's industrial estate in the 1990s testifies to this tendency. The material and emotional effects of capitalist industrialization are so profound that only the supernatural can bring security and relief. The rise of Hindu orthodoxy in India since Independence and the BJP in the 1980s may support this. Anyhow, local capitalist industrialization did not produce long-term social dislocation and disenchantment.

South Asians are not the only people who cling to their cultural and religious institutions during the early decades of capitalist industrialization. In Europe, the Dutch did the same during the period 1850-1950. They formed blocs 'defined by their religion or *Weltanschauung*' (Goudsblom, 1968: 31), like orthodox Calvinists and Roman Catholics. These blocs of the population, called pillars (*zuilen*) 'strove for fuller participation in society' and played an important political role. But the phenomenon of pillarization (*verzuiling*) was by no means confined to politics (Goudsblom: 32). Since the beginning of capitalist industrialization Dutch industrial workers have been organized according to religious beliefs. Unlike 'general', socialist trade unions, confessional unions 'took a subdued and generally conservative stand' (Goudsblom: 106). In 1963, 45 per cent of organized workers were members of confessional unions (Lijphart: 41); disenchantment of Dutch industrial workers was not spectacular during the first century of their existence.

The third manifestation of capitalist modernity is increased objectivization of labour relations in south Gujarat between 1970 and 2000. The enlarged scale of the enterprises and industrial operations prevents personal recruitment and control of workers. Moreover, the younger generation of owners and managers do not want the burden of personal relations. They prefer machines because workers mean problems. Last but not least, the rise of the specialized labour contractor made recruitment and control of workers a rewarding occupation and an 'external' responsibility.

NOTES

1. The prominence of Jain and Vaishnava Banias in the organization of pre-machine textile industry and their major role in the emerging manufacturing industry from 1880 onwards is the long-term continuity. Short-term continuities pertain to the involvement of local petty-producers such as artisans like Suthars, Luhars, Kumbhars and Kansaras, and people with a solid agricultural base such as Anavil Brahmins. Artisans could benefit from their skills, state-sponsored industrialization, and Green Revolution. Anavils took advantage of their influence and finance.
2. In The Netherlands the first spinning mill opened in 1830 (Brugmans, 1983: 75).
3. Reiniche (1996: 124, 148) found the same among residents of the small town of Tiruchendu in Tamil Nadu. It is a taluka headquarters with 70,000 inhabitants in 1991.

Bibliography

Alavi, Hamza (1964), 'Imperialism, Old and New', *Socialist Register*, London.

——— (1972), 'The State in Post-colonial Societies', *New Left Review*, no. 74.

Anderson, B.R.O.G. (1992), *Long-distance Nationalism: World Capitalism and the Rise of Identity Politics*, Amsterdam: Centre for Asian Studies Amsterdam.

Asaramji Maharaj, Swaminarayan Shri (1995a), *The Vedantic Message of Fearlessness*, Sabarmati, Ahmedabad: Sant Sri Asaramji Ashram.

——— (1995b), *Glory of Eternal Youth*, Sabarmati, Ahmedabad: Sant Shri Asaramji Ashram.

Bailey, F.G. (1969), *Stratagems and Spoils: A Social Anthropology of Politics*, Oxford: Blackwell.

Baran, Paul A. (1968), *The Political Economy of Growth*, New York: Monthly Review Press.

Barrington, Moore (1966), *Social Origins of Dictatorship and Democracy: Lord and Peasant in the Making of the Modern World*, Boston: Beacon Press.

Basham, A.L. (1954), *The Wonder that was India*, New York: Macmillan.

Benedict, Ruth (1946), *The Chrysanthemum and the Sword*, Boston: Houghton, Mifflin Company.

Beteille, Andre (1965), *Caste, Class, and Power: Changing Patterns of Stratification in a Tanjore Village*. Berkeley: University of California Press.

——— (1996), 'Caste in Contemporary India', in C.J. Fuller (ed.), *Caste Today*, Bombay: Oxford University Press.

Bettelheim, Charles (1971), *India Independent*, New York: Monthly Review Press.

Bleek, Wolf (1978), 'Achter de Coulissen van Antropologisch Veldwerk', in Ghana, Assen: Van Gorcum.

Boeke, J.H. (1946), *Oosterse economie*, Den Haag: Servire.

Boissevain, J.F. (1968), *Netwerken en Quasi Groepen: Enkele Beschouwingen over de Plaats van Niet-Groepen*, Assen: Van Gorcum.

——— (1974), *Friends of Friends, Networks, Manipulators and Coalitions*, Oxford: Blackwell.

Bombay Act LXXIX of 1948, The Bombay Shop and Establishment Act 1948 (1972), Bombay.

Breman, Jan (1974), *Patronage and Exploitation: Changing Agrarian Relations in South Gujarat, India*, Berkeley: University of California Press.

——— (1975), *The Market for Non-agrarian Labour in South-Gujarat, India*, Rotterdam: CASP Publications.

——— (1976), *Een Dualistisch Arbeids-bestel? Een Kritische Beschouwing van het Begrip de Informele Sector*, Rotterdam: Van Gennep.

——— (1978), 'Seasonal Migration and Cooperative Capitalism: The Crushing of Cane and Labour by the Sugar Factories of Bardoli, South Gujarat', *The Journal of Peasant Studies,* 1(6), pp. 41-70 and 2 (6), pp. 188-201.

——— (1979), 'The Market for Non-Agrarian Labour: The Formal versus Informal Sector', in S. Devadas Pillai and C. Baks (eds.), *Winners and Losers: Styles of Development and Change in an Indian Region*, Bombay: Popular Prakashan.

——— (1985a), 'Between Accumulation and Immiseration: The Partiality of Fieldwork in Rural India', *The Journal of Peasant Studies*, vol. 13, no. 1.

——— (1985b), *Of Peasants, Migrants and Paupers: Rural Labour Circulation and Capitalist Production in West India,* Delhi: Oxford University Press.

——— (1996), *Footloose Labour: Working in India's Informal Sector,* Cambridge: Cambridge University Press.

——— (1993), 'Anti-Muslim Pogroms in Surat', *Economic and Political Weekly*, vol. 28, no. 16, 17 April, pp. 737-41.

Breman, Jan and Enno. W. Hommes (1979), *Social Change in South Gujarat: An Introduction,* in S. Devadas Pillai and C. Baks (eds.), *Winners and Losers: Styles of Development and Change in an Indian Region*, Bombay: Popular Prakashan.

Brunt, Lodewijk (ed.) (1977), *Anders Bekeken: Wet en Werkelijkheid in Sociaal Onderzoek*, Meppel: Boom.

Buchanan, D.H. (1966), *The Development of Capitalist Enterprise in India*, New York: Kelley.

Census of 1971 (1972), Series 5, Gujarat, Valsad District, parts X-A and B, Ahmedabad.

——— (1972), Series 5, Gujarat, Valsad District, parts X-C-1, Ahmedabad.

——— 1981 (1983), General Population Tables, Primary Census Abstracts, part II-B, Ahmedabad.

Chaudhuri, K.N. (1990), *Asia before Europe: Economy and Civilization of the Indian Ocean from the Rise of the Islam to 1750*, Cambridge: Cambridge University Press.

Chua, Cathy (1986), 'Development of Capitalism in Indian Agriculture: Gujarat 1850-1900', *Economic and Political Weekly*, vol. 21, no. 48, 29 November, pp. 2092-9.

Cohn, B.S. (1968), *'Notes on the History of the Study of Indian Society and Culture'*, in M. Singer and B.S. Cohn, *Structure and Change in Indian Society*, Chicago: Aldine Publishing Company.

——— (1970), 'Society and Social Change under the Raj', *South Asian Review*, vol. 4, no. 1.

——— (1987), *An Anthropologist among the Historians and Other Essays*, Delhi: Oxford University Press.

Dandekar, V.M and N. Rath (1971), 'Poverty in India', *Economic and Political Weekly*, vol. VI, nos. 1 and 2, 2 and 9 January, Bombay.

Desai, Kiran (1995), *Nature and Conditions of Workers in Small Scale Industrial Workers in Gujarat*, Surat: Centre for Social Studies.

Dale, Stephen Frederic (1994), *Indian Merchants and Eurasian Trade*, Cambridge: Cambridge University Press.

Dobb, Maurice (1967), *Studies in the Development of Capitalism*, London: Routledge & Keagan Paul.

Dube, Leela (1996), 'Caste and Women', in M.N. Srinivas (ed.), *Caste; Its Twentieth Century Avatar*, Delhi: Penguin Book, pp. 1-27.

Dumont, L. (1970), *Homo Hierachicus: The Caste System and its Implications*, London: Weidenfeld & Nicholson.

Economist (2001), vol. 359, issue 8224.

Elder, J.W. (1959), 'Industrialisation in Hindu Society: A Case study in Social Change', Ph.D. thesis, Cambridge, Mass: Harvard University.

Elias, N. (1969), *Über den Prozess der Civilization*, Soziogenetische und Psychogenetische Untersuchungen, Bern: Francke Verlag, Munchen.

Employees' Provident Funds Act 1952 and thc Employees' Provident Funds' Scheme 1952 (1966), Delhi.

Epstein, T. Scarlett (1962), *Economic Development and Social Change in South India*, Manchester: Manchester University Press.

Factories Act 1948 (1973), Bombay.

——— (1997), Delhi: Universal Law Publishing Pvt. Ltd.

Farooqui, Amar (1996), 'Urban Development in a Colonial Situation: Early 19th Century Bombay', *Economic and Political Weekly*, vol. 31, no. 40, pp. 2746-59.

Frank, Andre Gunder (1967), *Capitalism and Underdevelopment in Latin America, Historical Studies of Chile and Brazil*, New York: Monthly Review Press.

——— (1969), *Latin America, Underdevelopment or Revolution*, New York: Monthly Review Press.

——— (1998), *Re-Orient: Global Economy in the Asian Age*, Berkeley: University of California Press.

Fox, Richard G. (1969), *From Zamindar to Ballot Box: Community Change in a North Indian Market Town*, Ithaca: Cornell University Press.

——— (1973), 'Pariah Capitalism and the Traditional Indian Merchants, Past and Present', in Milton B. Singer, *Entrepreneurship and Modernization of Occupational Cultures in South Asia*, Durham: Duke University.

Fuller, C. (1989), 'British India or Traditional India? Land, Caste and Power', in H. Alavi and J. Harriss, *Sociology of Developing Societies in South Asia*, Hampshire: Macmillan Education Ltd.

Fuller, C.J. (1996), 'Introduction: Caste Today', in C.J. Fuller (ed.), *Caste Today*, Bombay: Oxford University Press.

Gadgil, D.R. (1973), *The Industrial Evolution of India in Recent Times, 1860–1939*, Delhi.

GBS I (1923), *Gazetteer of the Baroda State, General Information*, vol. I, Bombay.

——— (1923), *Gazetteer of the Baroda State*, vol. II, Bombay.

Geertz, Clifford (1963), *Peddlers and Princes: Social Change and Economic Modernization*, Chicago: University of Chicago Press.

Gerth, H.H. and C. Wright Mills (1958), *From Max Weber: Essays in Sociology*, New York: Oxford University Press.

Ghurye, G.S. (1969), *Caste and Race in India*, Bombay: Popular Prakashan (first published in 1932, London: Routledge and Kegan Paul).

Goheen, Johan, M.N. Srinivas, D.G. Karve, and Milton Singer (1958), 'India's Cultural Values and Economic Development: A Discussion', *Economic Development and Cultural Change*, vol. 7, no. 1.

GIDC (1971), *Annual Report 1971*, Ahmedabad: Gujarat Industrial Development Corporation.

Gokhale, Balkrishna Govind (1979), *Surat in the Seventeenth Century: A Study in Urban History of Pre-modern India*, Bombay: Popular Prakashan.

Goody, Jack (1996), *The East in the West*, Cambridge: Cambridge University Press.

Gopal, Surendra (1975), *Commerce and Crafts in Gujarat, 16th and 17th Centuries: A Study in the Impact of European Expansion on Precapitalist Economy*, Delhi: People's Publishing House.

Gorter, Pieter (1994), 'The Rise of a New Class of Indian Industrialists: Economic and Political Networks on an Indian Industrial Estate', Universiteit van Amsterdam, Ph.D. thesis.

GSGSD (1962), *Gujarat State Gazetteers, Surat District*, Ahmedabad.

Goudsblom, Johan (1968), *Dutch Society*, New York: Random House.

Gough, Kathleen and Hari P. Sharma (eds.) (1973), *Imperialism and Revolution in South Asia*, New York: Monthly Review Press.

Hagen, E.E. (1962), *On the Theory of Social Change*, New York: Feffer & Simons.

Hardiman, David (1990), 'Penetration of Merchant Capital in Pre-colonial Gujarat', in Ghanshyam Shah (ed.), *Capitalist Development: Critical Essays—Felicitation Volume in Honour of Prof. A.R. Desai*, Bombay: Popular Prakashan.

——— (1984), 'Adivasi Assertion in South Gujarat: The Devi Movemement', in Ranajit Guha, *Subaltern Studies III: Writings on South Asian History and Society*, Delhi: Oxford University Press.

——— (1985), 'From Custom to Crime: The Politics of Drinking in Colonial South Gujarat', in Ranajit Guha, *Subaltern Studies IV: Writings on South Asian History and Society*. Delhi: Oxford University Press.

——— (2002), 'Christianity and the Adivasis of Gujarat', in Ghanshyam Shah, Mario Rutten, Hein Streefkerk, *Development and Deprivation in Gujarat in Honour of Jan Breman*, Delhi: Sage.

Harriss, John (1982), *Studies of Small-Scale Enterprises and Urban Labour in South India*, Madras: Madras Institute of Development Studies.

Haynes, Douglas E. (1991), *Rhetoric and Ritual in Colonial India. The Shaping of a Public Culture in Surat City, 1852-1928*, Berkeley: University of California Press.

Hazlehurst, Leighton W. (1966), *Entrepreneurship and the Merchant Castes in a Punjabi City*, Durham, N.C.: Duke University.

Hirway, Indira (1995), 'Selective Development and Widening Disparities in Gujarat', *Economic and Political Weekly*, vol. 30, no. 41, 14 October, pp. 2603-18.

Hobsbawm, E.I. (1969), *Industry and Empire*, Hammondsworth: Penguin Books.

Holmström (1976), *South Indian Workers: Their Life and Their Work*, Cambridge: Cambridge University Press.

——— (1984), *Industry and Inequality: The Social Anthropology of Indian Labor*, Cambridge: Cambridge University Press.

Hoselitz, Bert F. (1960), *Sociological Aspects of Economic Growth*, New York: The Free Press of Glencoe.

——— (ed.) (1968), *The Role of Small Industry in the Process of Economic Growth*, The Hague: Mouton.

Husken, Frans (1988), *Een dorp op Java: Sociale Differentiatie in een Boerengemeenschap 1859-1980*, Overveen: Acasea, Hommes, Enno. W. (1970), *Over de Evaluatie van Plattelandsplanning in India*, Universiteit van Amsterdam.

Hommes, Enno W. and Nivedita Trivedi (1979), 'Functioning of the Labour-market for Local Graduates', in S. Devadas Pillai and C. Baks (eds.) *Winners and Losers: Styles of Development and Change in an Indian Region*, Bombay: Popular Prakashan.

Kapp, K. William (1963), *Hindu Culture, Economic Development, and Economic Planning in India,* Bombay: Asia Publishing House.

ILO (1976), *Employment, Growth and Basic Needs: A One-World Problem,* Geneva, ILO.

Joshi, Satyakam (1999), 'Tribals, Missionaries and Sadhus: Understanding Violence in the Dangs', *Economic and Political Weekly,* vol. 34, no. 37, 11 September, pp. 2667-75.

Kapadia, Karin (1999), 'Gender Ideologies and the Formation of Rural Industrial Classes in South India Today', in Jonathan Parry, Jan Breman and Karin Kapadia (eds.), *The Worlds of Indian Industrial Labour,* Delhi: Sage.

Kapadia, K.M. (1966), 'Industrial Evolution of Navsari', *Sociological Bulletin,* vol. 15, no. 1.

Kapadia, K.M. and S. Devadas Pillai (1972), *Industrialisation and Rural Society: A Study of Atul-Bulsar Region,* Bombay: Popular Prakashan.

Kennedy Jr. Robert E. (1965), 'The Protestant Ethic and the Parsis', in Neil J. Smelser (ed.), *Readings on Economic Sociology,* Englewood Cliffs: Prentice Hall.

Kerr, Ian J. (1995), *Building the Railways of the Raj,* Delhi: Oxford University Press.

Kobben, A.J.F. (1972), 'Sociale Wetenschappen en Ethiek', *Sociologische Gids,* 19(5-6), Meppel: Boom.

Kolenda, Pauline (1984), *Caste in Contemporary India: Beyond Organic Solidarity,* Jaipur: Rawat.

Kloos, Peter (1972), 'Marginaal', *Sociologische Gids,* 19(5-6), Meppel: Boom.

——— (1987), *Filosofie van de Antropologie,* Leiden: Martinus Nijhoff.

——— (1988), *Door het Oog van de Antropoloog: Botsende Visies bij Heronderzoek,* Muiderberg: Dick Coutinho.

Kooiman D. (1989), *Bombay Textile Labour, Managers, Trade Unionists and Officials 1918-1939,* Amsterdam: Free University Press.

Leach, E.L. (ed.) (1960), *Aspects of Caste in India, Ceylon and North-West Pakistan,* Cambridge: Cambridge University Press.

Lessinger, Johanna (1992), 'Nonresident Indian Investment and India's Drive for Industrial Modernization', in Michael L. Blim and Frances Abrahamer Rothstein (eds.), *Anthropology and the Global Factory: Studies of the New Industrialization in the Late Twentieth Century,* New York: Bergin & Garvey.

Levy, Marion J. Jr. (1966), *Modernization and the Structure of Societies: A Setting for International Affairs,* Princeton: Princeton University Press.

Locations of Industries in Gujarat State, 1975, 1980 and 1985, vol. 1 (1995), Gandhinagar: Directorate of Economics and Statistics of Gujarat.

Lijphart, Arend (1968), *Verzuiling, pacificatie en kentering in de Nederlandse politiek*, Amsterdam: De Bussy.

Mandelbaum, D.G. (1970), *Society in India*, vols. 1 and 2, Berkeley: University of California Press.

Mani, Sunal (1995), 'Economic Liberalisation and the Industrial Sector', *Economic and Political Weekly*, vol. 30, no. 21, 27 May, pp. M38-M50.

Marx, K. and Friedrich Engels (1969), *Selected Works*, Moscow: Progress Publishers.

Mayer, Adrian C. (1960), *Caste and Kinship in Central India: A Village and its Region*, Berkeley: University of California Press.

McClelland, D.C. (1976), *The Achieving Society*, New York: Irvington.

McClelland D.C. and David G. Winter (1969), *Motivating Economic Achievment*, New York: The Free Press.

Mehta, Makrand (1982), *The Ahmedabad Cotton Textile Industry: Genesis and Growth*, Ahmedabad: New Order Book Co.

Minimum Wages Act 1948 with the Gujarat Minimum Wages Rules 1961 (1967), Ahmedabad.

Moore, W.E. and A.S. Feldman (eds.) (1960), *Labour Commitment and Social Change in Developing Areas*, New York.

Morris, Morris D. (1960), 'The Labour Market in India', in Wilbert E. Moore and Arnold S. Feldman (eds.), *Labour Commitment and Social Change in Developing Areas*, New York.

——— (1965), *The Emergence of a Labour Force in India: A Study of the Bombay Cotton Mills 1854–1947*, Berkeley: University of California Press.

——— (1968), 'Towards a Reinterpretation of Nineteenth Century Indian Economic History', *The Indian Economic and Social History Review*, vol. 5, no. 1.

——— (1974), 'What is a Famine', *Economic and Political Weekly*, vol. 9, no. 44, 2 November, pp. 1855-64.

Myers, Charles A., Subbiah Kannappan (1970), *Industrial Relations in India*, London.

Moulik, T.K. and R. Moulik (1989), 'Structural Changes in Rural Economy–Gujarat', *Science and People*, August.

Mukhtyar, G.C. (1930), *Life and Labour in a South Gujarat Village*, Calcutta: Longmans, Green and Co.

Naipaul, V.S. (1977), *India: A Wounded Civilisation*, London.

——— (1990), *India: A Million Mutinies Now*, London: Heinemann.

Nieuwenhuys, Olga (1990), 'Angels with Callous Hands: Children's Work in Rural Kerala (India)', Ph.D. thesis, University of Amsterdam.

Noronha, Ernesto (1996), 'Liberalisation and Industrial Relations', *Economic and Political Weekly*, vol. 31, no. 8, 24 February, pp. L14-L20.

ODI (1989), 'India's Economy after the Elections', Briefing Paper, London: Overseas Development Institute.

Omvedt, Gail (1990), 'Twice born Riot against Democracy', *Economic and Political Weekly*, vol. 25, no. 14, 7 April, pp. 723-30.

Olden van, J.F. (1972), 'Antropologie en Ethiek: Geannoteerde Bibliografie', *Sociologische Gids*, 19(5-6), Meppel: Boom.

Panini, M.N. (1995), 'The Social Logic of Liberalisation', *Sociological Bulletin*, 44 (1).

——— (1996), The Political Economy of Caste', in M.N. Srinivas (ed.), *Caste: Its Twentieth Century Avatar*, Delhi: Viking.

Patel, Sujata (2003), 'Bombay and Mumbai: Identities, Politics, and Populism', in: Sujata Patel and Jim Masselos (eds.), *Bombay and Mumbai: The City in Transition*, Bombay: Oxford University Press.

Patel, Surendra J. (1991), 'Growing Regional Inequalities in Gujarat', *Economic and Political Weekly*, vol. 26, no. 26, 29 June, pp. 1618-23.

Payment of Bonus Act 1965 with the Payment of Bonus Rules 1965 (1972), Allahabad.

Peace, A. (1980), 'Structural Inequalities in a North Indian City', *Contributions to Indian Sociology*, vol. 14, no. 2.

Perlin, Frank (1983), 'Money-use in Late Pre-colonial India and the International Trade in Currency Media', in Frank Perlin, *Studies in Society and Economy in Late Pre-colonial India,* Ph.D. thesis, Rijksuniversiteit Leiden.

Pillai, S. Devadas (1976), *Rajahs and Prajas: A Princely State Then and Now,* Bombay: Popular Prakashan.

Pillai, S. Devadas and C. Baks (eds.) (1979), *Winners and Losers: Styles of Development and Change in an Indian Region*. Bombay: Popular Prakashan.

——— (1979), 'District Level Politics', in S. Devadas Pillai and C. Baks (eds.), *Winners and Losers: Styles of Development and Change in an Indian Region*, Bombay: Popular Prakashan.

Pradan, Basantha K. and M.R. Saluja (1998), 'Industrial Statistics in India: Sources, Limitations and Data Gaps', *Economic and Political Weekly*, vol. 33, no. 21, 23 May, pp. 1263-70.

Punalekar, S.P. (1980), 'A Descriptive Study of Dhodias of Surat City', Surat: Centre for Social Studies.

Radhakrishna, R. (2002), 'Agricultural Growth, Employment and Poverty: A Policy Perpective', *Economic and Political Weekly*, vol. 37, no. 3, 19 January, pp. 243-50.

Raheja, Gloria Goodwin (1988), *The Poison in the Gift: Ritual, Presentation, and the Dominant Caste in a North Indian Village*, Chicago and London: The University of Chicago Press.

Ramaswamy, E.A. (1973), 'Politics and Organised Labour in India', *Asian Survey*, vol. XIII, no. 3.

——— (1974), 'The Role of the Trade Union Leader in India', *Human Organisation*, vol. 33, no. 2.

Reiniche, M.L. (1996), 'The Urban Dynamics of Caste: A Case Study from Tamilnadu', in C.J. Fuller (ed.), *Caste Today*, Bombay: Oxford University Press.

Rostow, W.W. (1960), *The Stages of Economic Growth*, Cambridge: Cambridge University Press.

Roy, Shibani and S.H.M. Rivzi (1985), *Dhodia Identity, Anthropological Approach*, Delhi: B.R. Publishing Corporation.

Rutten, Mario (1986), 'Social Profile of Agricultural Entrepreneurs: Economic Behaviour and Lifestyle of Middle Large Farmers in Central Gujarat', in *Economic and Political Weekly*, vol. 21, no. 13, 29 March, pp. A-15–A-23.

——— (1991), 'Capitalist Entrepreneurs and Economic Diversification: Social Profile of Large Farmers and Rural Industrialists in Central Gujarat, India', Ph.D. thesis, Universiteit van Amsterdam.

——— (1994a), *Farms and Factories: Social Profile of Large Farmers and Rural Industrialists in India*, Delhi: Oxford University Press.

——— (1994b), *Asian Capitalists in the Asian Mirror*, Amsterdam: CAS/VU University Press.

——— (2003), Azië van binnen en van buiten. Amsterdam: Vossiuspers UvA

Rutten, Rosanne (1990), *Artisans and Entrepreneurs in the Rural Philippines: Making a Living and Gaining Wealth in Two Commercialized Crafts*, Amsterdam: VU University Press.

Saberwal, S. (1976), *Mobile Man: Limits to Social Change in Urban Punjab*, Delhi: Vikas Publishing House.

——— (1977), 'Indian Urbanism: A Sociohistorical Perspective', *Contributions to Indian Sociology*, vol. 11, no. 1.

——— (1979), 'Sociologists and Inequality in India: The Historical Context', *Economic and Political Weekly*, annual number, vol. 14, nos. 7 and 8.

Said, E. (1978), *Orientalism*, New York: Random House.

Sandesara, J.C. (1988), 'Small-scale Industrialization: The Indian Experience', *Economic and Political Weekly*, vol. XXIII, no. 13.

Sau, Ranajit (1973), 'Growth and Fluctuation in the Indian Economy', *Economic and Political Weekly*, vol. 8, nos. 31-3, special number, August, pp. 1485-1500.

Sayer, Derek (1991), *Capitalism and Modernity: An Excursus on Marx and Weber*, London: Routledge.

Schendel, Willem van (1981), *Peasant Mobility. The Odds of Life in Rural Bangladesh*, Assen: Van Gorcum.

Schenk-Sandbergen, L. (1975), *Vuil werk, schone toekomst? He leven van straatvegers en vuilruimers, een onderzoek in Bulsar (India) en verkenningen in Peking, Shanghai, Tientsin en Tangshan (China)*, Amsterdam: Van Gennep.

Schenk-Sandbergen, Loes and Hans Schenk (1979), 'The Setting of Polarity: Introduction to the Research Area', in S. Devadas Pillai and C. Baks (eds.), *Winners and Losers: Styles of Development and Change in an Indian Region* Bombay: Popular Prakashan, pp. 18-38.

Scholte, Bob (1972), 'Toward a Reflexive and Critical Anthropology', in Dell Hymes (ed.), Reinventing Anthropology, New York: Pantheon Books (1st pub. 1969).

Scott, J.C. (1998), *Seeing Like a State: How Certain Schemes to Improve the Human Condition Have Failed*, New Haven and London: Yale University Press.

Shah, A.M. (1988), 'Rural-Urban Networks in India', *South Asia*, new series. vol. XI, no. 2.

——— (1982), 'Division and Hierarchy: An Overview of Caste in Gujarat' *Contributions to Indian Sociology*, no. 1, 16.

Shah, A.M. and I.P. Desai (1988), *Division and Hierarchy: An Overview of Caste in Gujarat*, Delhi: Hindustan Publishing Corporation.

Shah, Ghanshyam (1975), *Caste Association and Politial Process in Gujarat*, Bombay: Popular Prakashan.

——— (1987), 'Middle Class Politics: A Case of Anti-Reservation Agitations in Gujarat', *Economic and Political Weekly*, vol. 22, nos. 19, 20, 21, Annual Number, May, pp. 155-72.

——— (1993), 'Surat 1993', *Seminar*, 411, Nov.

Shah, Nandita and Nandita Gandhi (1998), 'Industrial Restructuring: Workers in the Plastic Processing Industry', *Economic and Political Weekly*, vol. 33, no. 22, 30 May, pp. L12-L20.

Sharma, Baldev R. (1969), 'The Indian Industrial Worker', *International Journal of Comparative Sociology*, vol. 10, March/June.

——— (1970), 'The Industrial Worker: Some Myths and Realities', *Economic and Political Weekly*, vol. 5, no. 22, 30 May, pp. 875-8.

——— (1974), *The Indian Industrial Worker: Issues in Perspective*, Delhi: Vikas.

Sheth, N.R. (1967), 'Society and Industrial Work in India: A Case Study', *Human Organisation*, vol. 26, spring/summer.

Singer, Milton B. (1966), 'Religion and Social Change in India: The Max Weber Thesis Phase Three', *Economic Development and Cultural Change*, vol. 14, no. 4.

Singh, V.B. (1973), *Wage Patterns, Mobility and Savings of Workers in India: A Study of Kanpur Textile Industry*, Bombay: Lalvani Publishing House.

Srinivas, M.N. (1962), *Caste in Modern India and Other Essays*, Bombay: Asia Publishing House.

——— (1979), 'Future of Caste', *Economic and Political Weekly,* annual number, vol. 24, nos. 7 and 8, Annual Number, February, pp. 237-42.

——— (1996), 'Introduction', in M.N. Srinivas, *Caste: Its Twentieth Century Avatar,* New Delhi: Viking.

Statistical Outline of Gujarat 1987 (1988), Gandhinagar: Directorate of Economics and Statistics, Government of Gujarat.

Statistical Outline of India 1989-90 (1989), Bombay: Tata Services Ltd.

Stouffer, Samuel A. (1949), *The American Soldier: Studies in Social Psychology in World War*, Princeton: Princeton University Press.

Streefkerk, Hein (1978), *Lichte Industrie in een Kleine Indiase Stad: Ondernemers en Arbeiders in Zuid-Gujarat sinds 1900,* Amsterdam: Universiteit van Amsterdam.

——— (1979), 'Small Entrepreneurs: Agents in Underdevelopment?' in Pillai and Baks, 1979.

——— (1985), *Industrial Transition in Rural India: Artisans, Traders and Tribals in South Gujarat*, Bombay: Popular Prakashan.

——— (1993), *On the Production of Knowledge*, Amsterdam: CAS/VU University Press.

——— (1997), 'Gujarati Entrepreneurship . . . Historical Continuity against Changing Perspectives', *Economic and Political Weekly,* vol. 32, no. 8, 22 February, pp. M2-M10.

Streefkerk-Hubbeling, Arni (1976), 'Inter (caste) Marriage: Intermixture of Power and Marginality', in S. Devadas Pillai (ed.), *Aspects of Changing India*, Bombay; Popular Prakashan.

——— (1979), 'Transformation and Accomodation: The Differential Meanings of Inter (Caste) Marriage', in S. Devadas Pillai and C. Baks (eds.), *Winners and Losers: Styles of Development and Change in an Indian Region*, Bombay: Popular Prakashan.

Spier, Fred (1996), *The Structure of Big History: From the Big Bang until Today,* Amsterdam: Amsterdam University Press.

——— (1999), *Geschiedenis in het Groot: Een alomvattende visie*, Amsterdam: Amsterdam University Press.

Subramanian, K.N. (1977), *Wages in India,* New Delhi: Tata McGraw-Hill.

Subramanian, Lakshmi (1988), 'Banias and the British: The Role of Indigenous Credit in the Process of Imperial Expansion in Western India in the Second Half of the Eigthteenth Century', *Modern Asian Studies*, 21, 3.

——— (1992), 'Western India in the Eighteenth Century', in Indu Banga (ed.), *Ports and Their Hinterlands in India*, Delhi: Manohar.

Thakore, G.D. (1979), 'A Portrait of Municipal Councillors', in S. Devadas Pillai and C. Baks (eds.), *Winners and Losers: Styles of Development and Change in an Indian Region*, Bombay: Popular Prakashan.

Tripathi, Dwijendra and Makrand Mehta (1990), *Business Houses in Western India: A Study in Entrepreneurial Responses 1850-1956*, Delhi: Manohar.

Tulpule, Bagaram (1971), 'Industrial Labour: A Privileged Class?', *Economic and Political Weekly*, vol. 6, no. 22, 29 May, pp. 1075-6.

UNESCO (1962), *Small-scale Industries and Social Change*, Delhi.

——— (1966), *Small Industries and Social Change, Four Studies in India* Delhi.

Unni, Jeemol (1998), 'Non-agricutural Employment and Poverty in Rural India', *Economic and Political Weekly,* vol. 33, no. 13, 28 March, pp. A36-A44.

Upadhya, C.B. (1988), 'The Farmer-Capitalists of Coastal Andra Pradesh', *Economic and Political Weekly,* vol. 23, no. 27, 2 July, pp. 1376-82.

Vijay, G. (1999), 'Social Security for Labour in New Industrial Towns', *Economic and Political Weekly,* vol. 34, no. 39, 25 September, pp. L10-L19.

Veen, Klaas W. van der (1969), *I Give Thee My Daughter: Marriage and Hierarchy among the Anavil Brahman of South Gujarat,* Assen: Van Gorcum, 1972.

——— (1975), 'The Joint Family: Persistence or Decay', in S. Devadas Pillai, *Aspects of Changing India*, Bombay: Popular Prakashan.

——— (1979), 'Urbanisation, Migration and Primordial Attachments', in S. Devadas Pillai and C. Baks (eds.), *Winners and Losers: Styles of Development and Change in an Indian Region*, Bombay: Popular Prakashan.

Veer, Peter van der (2003), 'Postmodern India', in Arvind Das and Marcel van der Linden (eds.), *Work and Social Change in Asia: Essays in Honour of Jan Breman*, Delhi: Manohar.

Vries, Jan de and Ad van der Woude (1995), *Nederland 1500-1815: De Eerste Ronde van Moderne Economische Groei*, Amsterdam: Uitgeverij Balans.

Wallerstein, I. (1974), '*The Modern World-System: Capitalist Agriculture and the Origins of the European World-Economy in the Sixteenth Century,* New York: Academic Press.

Weber, Max (1958), *The Religion of India*, Glencoe: The Free Press.

Wessel, Margit van (1998), 'Wealth and its Social Worth: Consumption and Morality in the Baroda Middle Class', paper presented at the

Conference on Commodities and Identities, ASSR, Universty of Amsterdam.

Wertheim, W.F. (1964), *East-West Parallels, Sociological Approaches to Modern Asia*. The Hague: W. van Hoeve Ltd.

Wolf, Eric R. (1982), *Europe and the People Without History*, Berkeley: University of California Press.

Young, F.W. (1971), 'A Macro Sociological Interpretation of Entrepreneurship', in Kilby. P. (ed.), *Entrepreneurship en Economic Development*, New York: Free Press.

Index